Wholeheartedness

The message of Haggai for today

Jonathan Griffiths

DayOne

© Day One Publications 2014

ISBN 978-1-84625-434-5

British Library Cataloguing in Publication Data available

Published by Day One Publications
Ryelands Road, Leominster, HR6 8NZ
Telephone 01568 613 740 FAX 01568 611 473
email—sales@dayone.co.uk
web site—www.dayone.co.uk
North America—email—usasales@dayone.co.uk

Cover design by Rob Jones, Elk Design
Printed by Orchard Press Cheltenham Ltd

Jonathan is the grandson of a preacher, a former pastor of the Metropolitan Tabernacle; preaching is obviously in his DNA. Here is a clear, careful, faithful and warm exposition of the short book of Haggai. Its importance for today belies its length, and Jonathan's analysis is both deeply encouraging and appropriately challenging. God's word through Haggai is still a message that Christians need to hear and act upon today. As you read, you will also learn how to understand old-covenant literature in the light of what Christ has done, so you may find yourself doubly blessed.

Adrian Reynolds, Director of Ministry, The Proclamation Trust, UK

The two short chapters of Haggai have a message that every Christian needs to know. When the first flush of excitement and joy in coming to know Christ begins to fade, or the necessary routine of life begins to rob Christ of his pre-eminence, then Haggai's message brings us back to first base: seek first the kingdom of God and his righteousness, and all else will be added. Jonathan Griffiths gives thoughtful attention to details in this Old Testament message without losing sight of the big picture applicable to New Testament Christians. The result is that readers' minds will be informed, their emotions stirred, and their wills challenged to realign their lives with God and his purposes.

Charles Price, Teaching Pastor at The Peoples Church, Toronto, Canada, convention speaker, and preacher on the Living Truth television and radio broadcasts

For my grandparents Gerald and Kitty Anna Griffiths

Contents

My first real encounter with the book of Haggai was at the 2011 Proclamation Trust Autumn Joint Ministers' conference where I found myself in the Haggai study group led by Simon Medcroft. Haggai was a book I did not know at all at the start of that conference but, over the course of three days, my eyes were opened to its arresting message and striking relevance to Christians today. I remain very grateful to Simon and the rest of that study group for their help in opening up this powerful book which had, until then, been very much a closed book for me.

It has been a privilege to preach and teach Haggai in a number of different contexts over the last three years, including at Christ Church, Westbourne, Grace Church, Dulwich, and the Cornhill Training Course. I have been thankful for the opportunity to open up this part of God's Word and to be sharpened, challenged and encouraged by the questions and feedback I have received. I am also very grateful to those who have helped me bring this book to completion. Adrian Reynolds, Charles Price and Andrew Wales provided perceptive and stimulating feedback on the manuscript; Vicky Nicholl and Suzanne Mitchell went through the text with a fine-tooth comb and made it immensely more readable. As ever, I am thankful to my wife, Gemma, without whose encouragement and patient support this little book would not have seen the light of day.

The Lord's stated aim in Haggai is to spur his people into action, to do the work that he has called them to do, 'that I may take pleasure in it and that I may be glorified' (Hag. 1:8). It is my prayer that this brief exposition of Haggai may prompt us as God's people to get on with the work he has graciously given us to do, for his pleasure and his glory.

For many of us, Haggai as a book is an entirely undiscovered country. It is small and easily overlooked, and it falls in a part of Bible history (the post-exilic period) that is relatively unknown. But even a brief dip into the book reveals that it is immensely contemporary and has a deeply challenging and wonderfully hope-filled message for believers today. The book of Haggai speaks to the people of God in an age of partial fulfilment of God's promises, when the work of the kingdom seems to be moving very slowly and unimpressively, and it calls God's people from self-centred half-heartedness to God-centred wholeheartedness, while revealing God's gracious plans to bless his people through the Lord Jesus.

The story of the situation of God's people Israel in Haggai's day really began in 599 BC when the great superpower of the day, the Babylonians, laid siege against Jerusalem. Judah was no match for the Babylonians, and the city soon fell; its walls were destroyed, its great temple reduced to ruins and many of its citizens carried off to exile in Babylon (the first wave of deportees leaving for Babylon in 597 BC). Although God sent this disaster upon his people for their unfaithfulness to him and his covenant (see Daniel's prayer of national repentance in Dan. 9), God had not forgotten his people and he was at work shaping international events for their salvation. In the year 539 BC Cyrus the Great of Persia captured Babylon and annexed it to his empire, and in 538 he issued a decree allowing the Jews to return to Jerusalem (Ezra 1–2).

Many of the Judeans who had settled in Babylon elected to stay there in the relative comfort and security of that great city rather than face the discomfort and dangers of rebuilding their lives in a ruined and defenceless city. But over forty thousand exiles did return when Cyrus made his extraordinary decree (Ezra 2:64–68). The challenges before them were immense: they needed to build homes and infrastructure to make Jerusalem habitable, they needed to rebuild the wall of the city to provide security, and, most importantly, they needed to rebuild the altar and the temple if they were to have access to God's presence and his forgiveness through the sacrificial system. Under the old covenant, God made himself available at the temple in Jerusalem; without the temple, the people's access to God was hampered and so their relationship with him was impaired. An unfinished temple, therefore, was not simply a practical inconvenience or a symbolic blemish; it constituted a spiritual crisis.

The early returnees recognized this priority and made it their business to get on with the work of rebuilding, and within about two years of their return they had laid the foundation of the temple (Ezra 3:10). However, opposition from hostile neighbours soon led to the project being derailed and work coming to a halt (Ezra 4), a situation that remained unchanged when Haggai arrived on the scene. The temple would not be completed until 515 BC, five years after Haggai's prophecy.

Haggai dates his ministry precisely to the 'second year of Darius the king' (1:1), which we know to be 520 BC. The messages contained in his book are delivered over four separate days: 29 August (the first day of the sixth month, 1:1), 21 September (the twenty-fourth day of the sixth month, 1:15), 17 October (the twenty-first day of the seventh month, 2:1), and 18 December (the twenty-fourth day of the ninth month, 2:10, 20).

Although the first returnees from Babylon got on with the work of rebuilding the temple with generosity and enthusiasm, by Haggai's day interest had waned. The people had, no doubt, been very discouraged by the opposition they faced in earlier days (Ezra 4). More than that, they had now been back in the land for eighteen years, and the great promises of restoration seemed to them unfulfilled. Eighteen years previously, the returnees would have travelled from Babylon to Judah with promises like those found in Isaiah 60 and 61 ringing in their ears:

Arise, shine, for your light has come,
    and the glory of the LORD has risen upon you …
And nations shall come to your light,
    and kings to the brightness of your rising …

Foreigners shall build up your walls,
  and their kings shall minister to you;
for in my wrath I struck you,
  but in my favour I have had mercy on you.
Your gates shall be open continually;
  day and night they shall not be shut,
that people may bring to you the wealth of the nations,
  with their kings led in procession.
For the nation and kingdom
  that will not serve you shall perish ...
(Isa. 60:1, 3, 10–12).

The people had returned to Judah with high expectations and filled with enthusiasm, but their hopes seemed to be disappointed. Yes, they had returned. Yes, God had moved the heart of Cyrus to allow them not only to return but also to rebuild the temple. But their situation was still one of humiliation under the Persians. The opening line of the book of Haggai is a painful reminder of that humiliation: while so much of the Bible is dated according to the reign of Israelite kings, Haggai is dated according to the rule of Darius, the Persian emperor. Added to that, the temple under construction in Jerusalem now seemed as 'nothing' (2:3) in the eyes of those who remembered the old one. Discouragement had soon given way to self-centredness; the people were busy feathering their own nests while the temple remained in ruins (1:3–5).

The LORD had graciously worked in the heart of Cyrus in keeping with his promise (Isa. 45:1) to allow the exiles to return to Judah. As Cyrus himself reported, God's purpose in prompting him to make that decree was that his house should be rebuilt:

Thus says Cyrus king of Persia: The LORD, the God of heaven, has given me all the kingdoms of the earth, *and he has charged me to build him a house at Jerusalem*, which is in Judah. Whoever is among you of all his people, may his God be with him, and let him go up to Jerusalem, which is in Judah, *and rebuild the house of the* LORD, the God of Israel—he is the God who is in Jerusalem. And let each survivor, in whatever place he sojourns, be assisted by the men of his place with silver and gold, with goods and with beasts, besides freewill offerings *for the house of God that is in Jerusalem* (Ezra 1:2–4, emphasis added).

God's grace in bringing about the return to Judah was intended to serve the purpose of his glory through the rebuilding of his house. There is an echo here of the intended purpose of the exodus many centuries before as God spoke to Moses: 'Then you shall say to Pharaoh, "Thus says the LORD, Israel is my firstborn son, and I say to you, 'Let my son go that he may serve me'"' (Exod. 4:22–23). Salvation was ultimately for the purpose of God's glory and not simply the people's pleasure. But as we see again and again throughout the Bible story, we sinful people so often take God's salvation and his grace and then use our freedom to serve our own agenda rather than God's. Once the initial thrill of freedom from slavery, captivity, exile and, ultimately, sin, has worn off, it's easy to turn to serving ourselves rather than God. And that is precisely what had happened here: 'Is it a time for you yourselves to dwell in your panelled houses, while this house lies in ruins?' (1:4).

As we have already seen, the temple stood at the heart of the spiritual life of the nation because it was the means by which the people's covenant relationship with God was maintained. To neglect the temple was to neglect God. That is why God's aim was not simply to get the people working on the temple (although he clearly did want that); his deeper aim was for the people to return to him (Hag. 2:17b; see also Zech. 1:3).

Haggai's message is timely for us today. It speaks to a people living in days of partial fulfilment of God's promises, when the progress of kingdom work seems slow, unexciting and unimpressive—to a people who have grown rather half-hearted when it comes to God's work, and in their discouragement have become increasingly worldly in their concerns. We today live a major stage on in salvation history from the people of Haggai's day, but we still live in days of partial fulfilment of God's promises. We are not in heaven yet. And the danger is that we can become discouraged, distracted and thoroughly half-hearted. So God through Haggai calls us to repent where we are guilty of neglecting the Lord, to return to him where we have drifted away, and get to work doing what he has given us to do.

Two particular challenges emerge in reading and applying Haggai today. The first comes in chapter 1 with the question of how to read and apply to our situation today the old-covenant curses that are operative in that chapter. The next challenge is how to trace the flow of logic in 2:5–19, where it is not immediately clear which periods of time the people are being invited to 'consider', nor why God chooses, rather surprisingly, to bless his people in verse 19. We will touch on these issues at the relevant points in Chapters 1 and 4, but they require some detailed discussion which is reserved for the 'Going Deeper' chapters at the end of the book. I hope that those chapters, where I try to outline some of my own work and theological reflection on the text, will be of particular value to those preparing to preach and teach Haggai.

The dangers of home improvement (1:1–11)

In the second year of Darius the king, in the sixth month, on the first day of the month, the word of the LORD came by the hand of Haggai the prophet to Zerubbabel the son of Shealtiel, governor of Judah, and to Joshua the son of Jehozadak, the high priest: 'Thus says the LORD of hosts: These people say the time has not yet come to rebuild the house of the LORD.' Then the word of the LORD came by the hand of Haggai the prophet, 'Is it a time for you yourselves to dwell in your panelled houses, while this house lies in ruins? Now, therefore, thus says the LORD of hosts: Consider your ways. You have sown much, and harvested little. You eat, but you never have enough; you drink, but you never have your fill. You clothe yourselves, but no one is warm. And he who earns wages does so to put them into a bag with holes.

'Thus says the LORD of hosts: Consider your ways. Go up to the hills and bring wood and build the house, that I may take pleasure in it and that I may be glorified, says the LORD. You looked for much, and behold, it came to little. And when you brought it home, I blew it away. Why? declares the LORD of hosts. Because of my house that lies in ruins, while each of you busies himself with his own house. Therefore the heavens above you have withheld the dew, and the earth has withheld its produce. And I have called for a drought on the land and the hills, on the grain, the new wine, the oil, on what the ground brings forth, on man and beast, and on all their labours.'

When is the right time to start a new evangelistic initiative? When is the right time to get going teaching the Bible to my children? When is the right time to increase my giving to gospel work? When is the right time to share the good news of Jesus with that neighbour, colleague or friend at school?

If you're anything like me, the instinctive answer to most of those questions will be 'soon', or 'when things settle down a bit', or 'when I've got my finances in order'. Those answers may seem really quite reasonable, given all that we've got going on in our busy lives and given all the demands on our money in tough times. But the problem with those kinds of answers, according to the prophet Haggai, is that God doesn't find them very impressive. As Haggai will show us, they betray a coolness of heart towards the Lord, and a deeper concern for our own comfort than for his work.

In the time of Haggai, the people of Jerusalem really had one main job to do for God: the task before them was to rebuild the temple that had been destroyed by the Babylonian invaders some years before. Eighteen years previously, forty thousand or so of the exiles had chosen to leave the comforts of the great city of Babylon to come back to a desolate Jerusalem. They came back single-minded in their devotion to the Lord's work and to the restoration of his house.

We read in the book of Ezra that these returning exiles gave generously in gold and silver to the temple rebuilding fund, and they got on with the work with energy and devotion. As we read the story in Ezra, we find that they started amazingly well. But once the foundations of the temple were relaid, the altar was rebuilt and sacrifices recommenced, opposition to the work soon came in, other concerns took priority, and the people lost their drive and determination. Eighteen years after the return, when Haggai prophesied to the people in 520 BC, the temple remained unfinished and the people uninterested: 'These people say the time has not yet come to rebuild the house of the LORD' (1:2). Notice that the people were not saying that they had given up on the building project. They had not declared that they had abandoned God's work altogether. They were simply saying that the time wasn't quite right.

'When I've got the renovations finished on my house, then I'll give.' 'When I've got my kids through school, then I'll make God's house a priority.' 'When I've made my pension contribution this year, then I'll write a cheque.' 'When I've got my career on track, then I'll make time.' But God isn't impressed, and in verse 4 he asks the kind of question that quickly turns our faces red and makes us long for a change of subject: 'Is it a time for you yourselves to dwell in your panelled houses, while this house lies in ruins?' When is it the right time to get on with the work that God has given us to do?

It is worth registering, right at the outset, that the work that God has given us to do *today* is not the same as the work he gave his ancient people to do *then*, all those years ago. In *that time and place*, the main assignment for God's people in Jerusalem was to get the ruined temple rebuilt. It was an urgent assignment: under the old covenant, God met with the people at the temple through his priests and made himself available there. Most crucially, forgiveness of sin was made possible through the sacrifices offered at the temple (albeit as an interim measure; see Heb. 10:4). The temple building was absolutely central to God's relationship with his people.

But an earthly temple building is, of course, no longer relevant today. We now meet with God through the Lord Jesus, who 'dwelt [or 'tabernacled'] among us' (John 1:14) and is himself the fulfilment of all that the old temple pointed towards (see, for instance, John 2:18–22). More than that, we learn that Christian believers, who are frequently described as being 'in Christ' and joined to him by his Spirit, are part of his 'body' (1 Cor. 12:12–31). God's interest now is not in a physical temple, but rather in his 'spiritual house' (1 Peter 2:4–5)—that is, his saved people, his church. God is building his spiritual house as he brings more and more people to salvation through faith in Jesus. Thrillingly, you and I participate in that great building project as we obey the Great Commission to 'go and make disciples of all nations' (Matt. 28:16–20).

As God builds his spiritual house, we have the privilege of assisting him through spreading far and wide the good news of Jesus.

That is our assignment. If we know and believe the gospel message for ourselves, we know just how urgent is the work before us. It's urgent because the gospel message is, quite simply, a matter of life and death. It's the message that, although we human beings deserve the judgement of eternal death for our wilful rebellion against the God who made us, Jesus, God's own Son, has died in our place and, through his death and resurrection, offers us forgiveness and the hope of eternal life. Added to the urgency of God's work from the human side, even more significant is the importance of it for God's own sake. Notice the reason that God gives for the people to get on with the work in verse 8: '... build the house, that I may take pleasure in it and that I may be glorified'.

The people of Haggai's day hadn't turned against God in open rebellion, as some of their ancestors had; but they had lost their zeal for God's work, and they were half-hearted in their devotion to him and to his honour. They were thoroughly distracted by the concerns of everyday life. As God addresses this half-hearted and distracted people in Haggai 1, he has for them a question, and then two instructions. As a people who are so often half-hearted and easily distracted ourselves, we need to listen carefully to what God has to say.

The LORD's question

Then the word of the LORD came by the hand of the prophet Haggai: 'Is it a time for you yourselves to dwell in your panelled houses, while this house remains a ruin?' (1:3–4).

Jerry the Jerusalemite walks through the front door with a massive sigh of relief. He has spent the last hour standing in the pouring rain while the priest performed the daily sacrifice down at the altar at the ruined temple.

It's been a foul day and the rain has been coming in sideways. Jerry, along with everyone else, is soaked through.

'No matter,' Jerry tells himself, 'at least I'm home now, where it's warm and dry.' He takes off his soaking coat and hangs it on the hook next to the big Aga range cooker in the kitchen. He and Becky have just had it installed during their kitchen refit and *it is a beauty*—four ovens, more hobs and plate-warmers than you know what to do with, baby blue in colour, gas-fired, and top of the range. After another satisfying gaze at the new Aga, Jerry nips into his freshly built sauna room to dry off and warm up properly. After that, he fully intends to settle into the deep calf-skin sofa down in the basement home theatre for a quiet evening in with Becky.

You see, Jerry the Jerusalemite and Becky his wife have spent the eighteen years since they returned to Jerusalem making the old family house—which had been left in ruins when the Babylonians finished with it—into the dream home they had always longed for. The unpleasantness of standing outside in the rain for that long hour earlier in the day reminded Jerry that *it might be time, before too long*, to make that donation to the temple fund, and perhaps even to offer a bit of his own time to the reconstruction project. 'Yes, when the interior decorator is all finished and her bill is paid, the temple fund will definitely be the next thing on the list.'

One of the striking things about the situation Haggai reports is how much the people and their priorities have changed over the period of eighteen years since their return. When the exiles first returned from Babylon to Jerusalem, they had been wholehearted in their commitment to the task God had given them and they had been hugely generous in their support of it. Notice what Ezra reports of those early days: 'Some of the heads of families, when they came to the house of the LORD that is in Jerusalem, made freewill offerings for the house of God, to erect it on its site. According to their ability, they gave to the treasury of the work

61,000 darics of gold, 5,000 minas of silver, and 100 priestly garments' (Ezra 2:68–69). I looked up the price of gold and silver on the London market recently, and 61,000 darics, or 500 kilos of gold, at last check, is worth about £12,700,000. And 5,000 minas, or 3 tonnes, of silver is worth about £1,100,000.

When the exiles returned to the land, with all the uncertainties of life in a ruined city before them, they gave the equivalent of nearly £14 million into the temple rebuilding fund. They gave generously, perhaps even recklessly, to the work that God had set before them. That was eighteen years before, but then came the hard realities of life: houses to build and maintain, children to educate, a future to plan for. The priorities of home, family and the normal things of life took over, and the temple never even got off the ground.

There were two things that the people of Jerusalem needed to give in order to see the temple built—and they're the same two things you and I have at our disposal to give to gospel work now: *money* and *time*. That's really all there is; there is *money* to pay for others to do the work and to buy the equipment, and there is *time* for us to roll up our own sleeves and get stuck in, and to pray for the work as well.

I wonder if there was a stage in your life when you would have made decisions and sacrifices for the gospel that, humanly speaking, were reckless, costly and impractical? Perhaps they were decisions about finance, career, home and family. Perhaps they were costly sacrifices of time and money, but sacrifices that you made gladly because the gospel was at the top of your priority list. Was there a stage in your life when you were wholehearted in your commitment to the gospel like that? Maybe your heart is still like that today. Praise God if it is. But perhaps for you it was when you were at college, when you decided to set aside or limit ambitions for a lucrative career and instead thought through where you could be most useful for the kingdom. Perhaps it was in the earlier days of family life, when you went without things at home in order to give to strategic gospel work.

But then came the mortgage, or perhaps just the bigger mortgage. Then came the pressure at work and the opportunity for promotion, and the need to spend more hours at the desk. Then came fees for children's education. Then came the need to save and to build up the pension pot. Then came the awareness of ageing and the lack of energy to take on extra things at church. Then came the relief of retirement, and the longing just to enjoy a bit more time to do the things there had never been time to do before. And suddenly the work of the gospel, which once was high up on your agenda, was much lower down. Suddenly the urgent work of spreading the good news of Jesus and teaching others to follow him—well, that work seems just a bit *less* urgent, next to all the *other* urgent things in life. And we tell ourselves that the time isn't quite right.

But God has an awkward question for us: 'Is it a time for you yourselves to dwell in your panelled houses, while this house lies in ruins?' (1:4). Is it a time for us to invest more and more time and money in our homes, our futures, our careers and our own personal and domestic pursuits, while many in our community and in our world know nothing of the Lord Jesus Christ? Is it a time to feather your nest so industriously while so much gospel work remains unfinished?

That's the LORD's question, and it's not an entirely comfortable one to consider. Now we move on to his two instructions for us.

The LORD's first instruction

Thus says the LORD of hosts: Consider your ways. You have sown much, and harvested little. You eat, but you never have enough; you drink, but you never have your fill. You clothe yourselves, but no one is warm. And he who earns wages does so to put them in a bag with holes (1:5–6).

It's a Saturday morning, 520 BC, and Jerry the Jerusalemite sits down with his morning coffee and unfolds his copy of *The Jerusalem Gazette*. The headlines are familiar: 'Inflation Hits 5 Per Cent'; 'Savings Melting Away'; 'Real Income Dropping'; 'Standards of Living Deteriorating'.

It all sounds very contemporary. The people of Jerusalem in Haggai's day weren't destitute; they ate and drank, and had clothes to wear (v. 6), and they even had panelled houses to live in (v. 4). But they were working hard to improve their lot in life, and were finding all the while that the tide was pushing in the opposite direction: 'he who earns wages does so to put them into a bag with holes' (v. 6).

Jerry mutters, 'Tell me about it—don't I know it' under his breath, folds the paper up again and tosses it down.

What's going on? Why are the people's efforts leading to frustration? Why are the people of Jerusalem giving every hour of the day over to work in the hope of reaping greater rewards, only to find that they're worse off than when they began? Verse 9 says, 'You looked for much, and behold, it came to little. And when you brought it home, I blew it away. Why? declares the LORD of hosts. Because of my house that lies in ruins, while each of you busies himself with his own house.'

The LORD invites his people in 520 BC— and us today—to 'consider our ways' (v. 7): that is, to look at our life situation, and to consider how things are going.

As we look at our hopes and dreams, is it just possible that we find that our strivings for material comfort at home, for success at work, for prosperity and for the increase of our standard of living are reaping less reward than we might have hoped? Or, if we are reaping a material reward, are we finding that those material prizes and badges of success are not bringing us the *satisfaction* and *fulfilment* that we might have expected? The people of Jerusalem were striving hard for those things, and they certainly were frustrated and dissatisfied. The LORD's very striking message to them was that he himself was holding back their success, and was doing so because their priorities were skewed.

Look how directly God had intervened to bring their ambitions to futility: 'Therefore the heavens above you have withheld the dew, and the earth has withheld its produce. And I have called for a drought on the land and the hills, on the grain, the new wine, the oil, on what the ground brings forth, on man and beast, and on all their labours' (vv. 10–11). If we set this description against the list of covenant curses in Leviticus 26 and Deuteronomy 28, we see that God has actually activated his covenant curses against his people for their disobedience as an act of discipline to bring them to their senses. God himself is frustrating their efforts in order to bring them to repentance.

Under the new covenant, we no longer fear God's covenant curses being exercised against us. The New Testament makes it clear that Jesus has died to bear the curse of the law for us and to make available to us the blessings of a right relationship with God (Gal. 3:13–14). But it is still the case that the sovereign Lord works through the circumstances of our lives to discipline us, to call us to repentance, and to train us in godliness (see Heb. 12:3–11).[1]

I wonder if you have ever had the frustrating experience of trying to drive your car with the handbrake on. Ours got jammed recently when we left the car at the airport while we were away on holiday, and it really was an inconvenience to arrive back after a long-haul flight with two tired children and find that the car refused to budge! God tells the Israelites here that he has put the brakes on their ambitions. He himself is holding them back and slowing them down. So if they're not realizing their materialistic dreams and not finding satisfaction in work, money and home, they are to know that God is applying the brakes in order to get their attention. He is pointing out to them that they have invested too much in the wrong things, and they have ignored what is of first-order importance. They have set him and his work to one side while they have got on with their own domestic plans and their own private ambitions. So he has activated his covenant curses against them so that they might repent of their selfishness and return to him.

He says to us as he says to them, 'Consider your ways.' Consider carefully whether the time you are ploughing into work and home, and the money you are investing in feathering your own nest, is reaping all the rewards you hoped it might. It may be that, in our individual circumstances, in all kinds of different ways, God has applied the brakes in order to discipline us, to get our attention, and to show us that we've invested too much in the wrong things.

'Consider your ways.' That's God's first instruction.

The LORD's second instruction

Go up to the hills and bring wood and build the house, that I may take pleasure in it and that I may be glorified, says the LORD (v. 8).

The LORD's second instruction is simply this: Get on with it; get to work at the job I've assigned you. Draw a line right through your 'To do' list, reorder it, and put my work at the top. That's the instruction, and it sounds simple enough. But if the people of Jerusalem are going to obey it, it's going to take a leap of faith. After all, we need to remember that they're facing *tough times*. Crops are poor, the economy is flagging, inflation is high and jobs are at risk. In times like that, everyone's natural instinct is to put in *more* hours at work, to save *more*, to invest *more*, to be *more* careful for the family finances. But in tough times, God says, put your career, your comfort and your financial security lower down your list and get on with the job I've given you to do. At a time when everyone else is investing more in shoring up their own financial position and securing their career, you and I are called upon to make the costly investment of pouring time and money into the work of the gospel in a sacrificial and uncalculating way.

One of the interesting features of Haggai is the name he uses for God. Time and time again (fourteen times in all), Haggai refers to God as 'the LORD of hosts' (vv. 2, 5, 7, 9, etc.), or, as other translations have it, 'the Lord Almighty' (see the NIV, for example). The name simply points to the fact that the LORD is the commander of heaven's armies. He has hosts of angels at his beck and call. He is the powerful one, the unstoppable one—the LORD Almighty.

I do not think there is anything random about that choice of name for God here. Through Haggai, God is calling us radically to reorder our priorities, to place our lives in his hands afresh, in lean times to give ourselves and our resources wholly over to his service—and then to trust him with the consequences. And the point is that we *can* trust him, because he is none other than the 'LORD of hosts', the powerful, unstoppable, almighty God of heaven and earth.

At its heart, the issue of Haggai 1 is a simple question of faith. Do we trust God to take care of us, or do we feel that we need to take care of number one because no one else will?

Statistics recently published show that overall charitable giving in the UK was down 20 per cent year on year;[2] I imagine that statistics throughout the Western world would show similar declines for recent years. Wouldn't it be wonderful if, in lean times, when charities all over the place are having to cut back on their activities for lack of resources, the church could be expanding into new areas of ministry and pressing ahead with fresh initiatives to reach the community with the good news because of the overwhelming generosity of God's people? When there is a general sense of weariness of doing good in society, wouldn't it be wonderful if we could buck the trend and add *more* energy, *more* time, *more* workers and *more* money to that Great Commission assignment in our local areas and to the ends of the earth?[3]

When is the right time to get on with the work of the gospel? At what stage should gospel priorities drive my money management and my time management? I'm afraid the answer is uncomfortably clear. And so I wonder if you and I are willing, today, to 'consider our ways'? Are we willing to look carefully at those two books that betray so quickly the state of our hearts before God—our diary and our chequebook—and to reorder our priorities to make sure that the work of the gospel is our top priority?

QUESTIONS FOR REFLECTION, DISCUSSION AND APPLICATION

1. In what areas of your life have you allowed personal, domestic and material concerns to squeeze out the work of the gospel?
2. Are you aware of ways that God may be at work in your circumstances to wake you up and call you back to wholehearted devotion to him and his work?
3. What are the practical changes and, perhaps, sacrifices you need to make in order to see the work of the gospel move forward?
4. Do you trust the LORD of hosts enough to make those changes?

NOTES

1 The keen-eyed reader will notice that this section of Haggai raises a major theological issue for believers today: how do we apply for ourselves Old Testament passages where God's covenant curses are operative? As noted above, Jesus has died to bear the curse of the law on our behalf (Gal. 3:13–14), and so believers today do not live in fear of God's curse. So, do passages such as Haggai 1 simply become a prompt for us to give thanks that we do not live under the fear of old-covenant curses? As with so many aspects of the old covenant as it relates to the new, we should expect to see elements of both continuity and discontinuity between the covenants. There is discontinuity because Jesus has become the curse for us, so that there is no curse left for the people of God. But there is continuity too, because part of God's original purpose in his covenant curses was to act in his sovereignty to discipline his people for their good in order to bring them to repentance (see Lev. 26:14–28, especially vv.

23–24, 28), a purpose which continues under the new covenant (as already noted, see Heb. 12:3–13). Therefore it is still appropriate to heed the call to 'consider your ways' and ask whether God is at work in his sovereignty to discipline us for our good. For a fuller discussion of how to read and apply today Old Testament passages that speak of God's covenant curses and blessings, see 'Going Deeper 1: Reading Old-Covenant Blessings and Curses Today'.

2 *UK Giving 2012: An Overview of Charitable Giving in the UK, 2011/12* (London/West Malling: National Council for Voluntary Organisations/Charities Aid Foundation, 2012), p. 4.

3 The big questions of how much to give and how to find the right balance between prudence and generosity are beyond the scope of this brief study. A helpful starting point on the biblical approach to giving is John Stott's little booklet *The Grace of Giving: 10 Principles of Christian Giving* (London/Oxford: Langham Partnership International/International Fellowship of Evangelical Students, 2004).

Getting the job done (1:12–15)

confession?

Then Zerubbabel the son of Shealtiel, and Joshua the son of Jehozadak, the high priest, with all the remnant of the people, obeyed the voice of the LORD their God, and the words of Haggai the prophet, as the LORD their God had sent him. And the people feared the LORD. Then Haggai, the messenger of the LORD, spoke to the people with the LORD's message, 'I am with you, declares the LORD.' And the LORD stirred up the spirit of Zerubbabel the son of Shealtiel, governor of Judah, and the spirit of Joshua the son of Jehozadak, the high priest, and the spirit of all the remnant of the people. And they came and worked on the house of the LORD of hosts, their God, on the twenty-fourth day of the month, in the sixth month, in the second year of Darius the king.

I n the previous chapter we looked at the challenging opening verses of Haggai, where God rebuked his people for ignoring the work that he had given them to do in rebuilding the temple while they merrily feathered their own nests and got on with their own domestic concerns. We felt the sting of that rebuke ourselves because we are often so slow to get on with our assignment today—the Great Commission to go and make disciples of all nations for the Lord Jesus—and we so easily devote much time and energy into making our own lives comfortable and prosperous. Haggai's opening message for us was clear enough. But as we reached the end of that first message at verse 11, I found myself in a quandary, and perhaps you did too.

I hear the LORD's rebuke from verses 1 to 11. I know that I don't give the time and energy to the gospel that I should, and I know that I'm far more concerned than I should be with my own comfort and private domestic concerns. But the problem is that, very often, in my heart of hearts, I'm not all that inclined to change—and I don't quite see *how* I will change.

Like the people of Jerusalem of Haggai's day who looked out at a massive building site before them, we today as followers of the Lord Jesus look out at big neighbourhoods, big cities, big counties and states, big countries, and a very big world to reach for him—and the job seems unimaginably huge. So, faced with such a big task, and knowing how unresponsive and self-interested my heart often is, I wonder, quite frankly, if the job will ever get done. How will God move a half-hearted people to get on with the work that he has given us to do?

Happily, that is the very issue addressed by these final verses of Haggai 1. They show us what God did to move an uninterested people from self-focused apathy to God-focused industry. In particular, they show us three essential elements that must be in place if God's work is to be completed. If the temple was to be built then, and the Great Commission is to be fulfilled now, these three elements must be in place: *the Word of God*, *the fear of God* and *the presence of God*.

The Word of God

Then Zerubbabel the son of Shealtiel, and Joshua the son of Jehozadak, the high priest, with all the remnant of the people, obeyed the voice of the LORD their God, and the words of Haggai the prophet, as the LORD their God had sent him (v. 12).

The turnaround that takes place here is remarkable. At the start of the chapter the people are carrying on as they have done for sixteen years; they are making a show of religion, but are actually prioritizing their own comfort and their own domestic pursuits. They are completely ignoring the work God has given them to do. At the start of the chapter, the temple building lies in ruins and the people are distracted and thoroughly uninterested. But by the end of the chapter, all that has changed. The LORD has sent his prophet to rebuke the people and to call them to get on with the job, with the result that the whole community 'obeyed the voice of the LORD their God' and 'came and worked on the house of the LORD of hosts, their God' (v. 14).

What has prompted the 180-degree turn? What has transformed the situation? In the first instance it has been the Word of God.

That fact probably shouldn't surprise us. Think about some of the things the Bible itself says about the power of the Word of God. Think right back to the beginning of the Bible story, to the creation of the world. How did God do it—how did he make something from nothing, a world from a void? He spoke: '"Let there be light", and there was light ... "Let there be an expanse in the midst of the waters ..." And it was so' (Gen. 1:3–7). 'Let there be ... Let there be ... And it was so.'

Not only did God make the world by his Word, but he also sustains the world by his Word. We are told in Hebrews 1 that the Lord Jesus Christ upholds the universe by his powerful Word (Heb. 1:3). That's the big, cosmic picture. But God's Word is powerful to change individual lives as well. The apostle Peter writes in 1 Peter that Christian believers have been 'born again ... through the living and abiding word of God' (1 Peter 1:23). God brings spiritually dead people to life through his living Word.

In light of the Bible's presentation of the power of God's Word, it follows that if we want to see progress and change in our own spiritual lives, we need to put the Word of God at the centre of our personal lives, our family lives and our lives together as the people of God. Time spent reading God's Word regularly on our own is not wasted time, and it will bear fruit. Time spent with our children and as a family in the Word of God will do us good and must not be neglected. Our churches need to have the Word of God at the centre of all that we do. The preaching of the Word of God at the main weekly gathering should be the 'main event' in the church's calendar. Along with that, prioritizing other occasions during the week when the church family gathers around the Word to hear God's voice is essential to the church's vitality.

I imagine that you are probably already convinced of the power of God's Word (given the time you are investing in getting to grips with the message of Haggai). But if we are already convinced, if we are already trying to prioritize the Word in our personal lives, and if we are already part of Word-centred churches, Haggai challenges us to think personally for a moment and ask ourselves whether we're *actually listening* to God's Word as we hear it. We need to consider that challenge because it is perfectly possible to be exposed to God's Word regularly, but actually to be ignoring it completely. The danger is perhaps especially acute when it comes to hearing the preached Word of God.

It is possible for us—in fact, it is terrifyingly easy for us—to *ignore* the preaching that we hear week by week. We can be physically present on a Sunday, and we can hear what is being said by the preacher, but we can find ourselves allowing it to go in one ear and out of the other. We'll know we're doing that if we find ourselves constantly *evaluating* the sermon (how zippy was it, how easy to listen to, how brief, how well illustrated?) but very rarely seeking to apply it to ourselves and respond to it personally. We so easily become sermon *critics* and even sermon *connoisseurs*, rather than sermon *hearers*.

But notice how the people hear and receive the prophet Haggai's message in verse 12: the people 'obeyed the voice of the LORD their God, and the words of Haggai the prophet, as the LORD their God had sent him'. As they gathered together and listened to the man in front of them, the people of Jerusalem recognized that they were not simply hearing a human voice, but they were hearing God's voice. They recognized that God had sent Haggai because Haggai was speaking God's Word, and so they listened to his voice as though it were God's voice. And they obeyed.

Now, there are clear and significant differences between preachers today and biblical prophets. Preachers today are not writing Scripture and bringing fresh revelation. But when a preacher stands up before God's assembled people and faithfully says what God's Word is saying, God's own voice is heard.[1] And if we know that God's Word has been faithfully proclaimed, our primary responsibility is not to *critique*, but to *obey*.

Are you a sermon critic and evaluator, or a sermon hearer and even a sermon obey-er? I know from my own heart and experience how easy it is to be the former, and how hard it is to be the latter; but Haggai shows us afresh how vital it is to receive the words of God's spokesmen as his words and so to listen and respond.

This, then, is the first essential that must be in place if the work of God is to be done: the Word of God, and particularly the preached Word of God. If we want to be changed and moved to obedience to get on with the gospel work before us, we need to be hearing and heeding God's Word individually, as families, and as church families.

The fear of God

Then Zerubbabel the son of Shealtiel, and Joshua the son of Jehozadak, the high priest, with all the remnant of the people, obeyed the voice of the LORD their God, and the words of Haggai the prophet, as the LORD their God had sent him. And the people feared the LORD (v. 12).

The year is 1980 or thereabouts, and it's a pleasant early autumn day in the city of Cambridge. An eighteen-year-old boy—we'll call him Michael—arrives at the gate of Selwyn College for his first term at the university. The place is swarming with people. Michael's slightly pushy mother wanders over to the porter's lodge, finds a modestly dressed older man standing outside, and asks him if he would mind giving a hand with the luggage. She leads him over to the family estate car, opens up the boot, points at the big trunk inside, and the older man and her rather embarrassed son meekly lug the great trunk up the winding staircase and into Michael's new room.

His mother says her goodbyes, and Michael unpacks one or two things and then heads to the afternoon reception for the new students. He and the others gather, chatting slightly nervously among themselves and waiting for the Master of the College—*the great man himself*—to arrive. Michael is rather perplexed when the elderly porter he met earlier enters the room and begins to address the assembled crowd. And then, in an awful moment of realization, it dawns on him: the elderly man whose services his mother had requisitioned was none other than the Very Reverend Owen Chadwick, Regius Professor of History, sometime President of the British Academy, Vice Chancellor of the University of Cambridge, and—particularly relevant for Michael's next three years—Master of Selwyn College.

It was a simple miscalculation on his mother's part, but a fairly disastrous one. The heart of it was that she had simply failed to identify properly the man in the bowler hat.

The end of verse 12 tells us that part of the reason why the people of God set aside their selfish interest in feathering their own nests and got back to the work of God was that they remembered again who God is. Evidently they had forgotten; but God, through his prophet, had reminded them, and now 'the people feared the LORD'.

To 'fear the LORD' means simply to recognize him for who he truly is. Fearing him is not about being terrified of him. It is about knowing that he is the God who made the world, rules the world and will judge the world, and so giving him the reverential respect and honour that are his due.

The sinful human heart will always tend to shrink God down to size. That's what had been happening for the last sixteen years in Israel. The people of Jerusalem had simply forgotten who God is and they had imagined that he was prepared to play second fiddle to their personal goals and ambitions. He was there to pray to if things got a bit rough, and there to offer sacrifices to when they felt guilty about their sin. Oh yes, God was there. But they had forgotten what kind of God he was.

They *must* have forgotten who God is if they were able to say the words of verse 2 for sixteen long years: 'the time has not yet come to rebuild the house of the LORD.' The question God put to them in verse 4 was acutely embarrassing: 'Is it a time for you yourselves to dwell in your panelled houses, while this house lies in ruins?' But the shocking thing was that they *did actually think* it was time for them to live in their panelled houses while God's house remained a ruin. This was because in their practical thinking (even if they would never have dared say it) they had come to view themselves as more important than God.

Another way of putting it—to borrow the language of verse 12—was that they had simply stopped '*fearing*' the LORD. Perhaps they imagined, as we sometimes do, that God was there simply to be their servant, to intervene when called upon to make their lives better. And they had forgotten that, in reality, *they* were there to serve him, to bring *him* the honour that is his due. But the LORD reminded them that the real priority was in fact his honour and his pleasure, and not their own. Remember the reason he gave them in verse 8 for getting on with the rebuilding: 'Go up to the hills and bring wood and build the house, *that I may take pleasure in it and that I may be glorified*' (emphasis added) That's what God says matters, and part and parcel of fearing him is sharing his priorities.

Perhaps the thing that most effectively woke up the people of Jerusalem and reminded them of the LORD's true power and identity was the message of verses 9–11. Here the LORD points out to the people that their crops have been really lacklustre of late and they've been struggling financially, and he tells them the true reason for their difficulties:

You looked for much, and behold, it came to little. And when you brought it home, I blew it away. Why? declares the LORD of hosts. Because of my house that lies in ruins, while each of you busies himself with his own house. Therefore the heavens above you have withheld the dew, and the earth has withheld its produce. And I have called for a drought on the land and the hills, on the grain, the new wine, the oil, on what the ground brings forth, on man and beast, and on all their labours (vv. 9–11).

As an act of discipline towards his people and in keeping with the promises of his Word, the LORD himself has called for a drought on the fields and the crops, the people and the livestock. He has the power to do that, and he is willing to use his power to get his people's attention and to call them back to himself. He is the 'LORD of hosts' or the 'LORD Almighty', as he is named throughout Haggai. He is the all-powerful LORD of heaven's armies, the one whose power is limitless and who must not be trifled with. Having been reminded of this, the people feared him once again.

I take it that, if you're a Christian believer, you would say that you fear the LORD. You recognize him for who he is. You know that he made you and will judge you, and so calls for your complete allegiance. But the sobering fact is that the people of Jerusalem of 520 BC would have said the same thing all the way along. They were God's people, after all. They were Israelites. *Of course* they feared God. Nonetheless, the reality was that for sixteen years they had forgotten what it meant to fear him, and they had been living as hypocrites. It was all too plain to see. Their priorities demonstrated in no uncertain terms their true attitude to God. They were treating him as their servant and not as their King. Their house came first. Their pleasure was paramount. Their own honour was the priority. And God's concerns came a long way down the list.

But when God brings his Word to bear upon the situation, the people see their error, and they learn again to fear the LORD. What was the proof that they feared him? The expression and proof of their fear of the LORD was their obedience to the voice of the LORD as they heard it in the prophet who delivered his Word (v. 12).

For the people's behaviour, obedience and service to be transformed, their attitude towards God had to be changed. The two went hand in hand.

If you and I are aware that we are not terribly inclined to get on with the work of making disciples of all nations; if we are not all that interested in talking to our friends about Jesus; if we are not all that motivated to encourage other believers to grow as disciples of Jesus; if we are not investing time and prayer in the spiritual nurture of our families; if our hearts are much more fired by pursuing our own private ambitions and our own domestic concerns—we need to ask ourselves if we've forgotten who God is.

Have we forgotten that he is our Creator and Sustainer who deserves our obedience and worship? Have we forgotten that he is our Saviour who deserves our deepest gratitude and highest praise? Have we forgotten that he is the sovereign, all-powerful LORD Almighty of heaven and earth who calls us to honour and obey him? Have we forgotten that he is our Judge who deserves our reverential fear?

The fear of the LORD is the second essential element that needs to be in place if God's work is to be completed.

The presence of God

Then Haggai, the messenger of the LORD, spoke to the people with the LORD's message, 'I am with you, declares the LORD.' And the LORD stirred up the spirit of Zerubbabel the son of Shealtiel, governor of Judah, and the spirit of Joshua the son of Jehozadak, the high priest, and the spirit of all the remnant of the people. And they came and worked on the house of the LORD of hosts, their God, on the twenty-fourth day of the month, in the sixth month, in the second year of Darius the king (vv. 13–15).

My wife and I have two young children. We take great delight in them, but like all parents, we sometimes find the privilege of parenting hard work. I think it is fair to say that the hardest part of the parenting day is bedtime. By that stage in the day our energy reserves are inevitably at a low ebb. What we long to do is to say to the children, 'Look, it is time for bath and bed. Could you please both make your way upstairs, run the bath, put your clothes in the laundry basket, brush your teeth, wash your hair, dry yourselves off, have a quick read of your Bible, say your prayers, get into bed—and we'll pop up in forty-five minutes and say goodnight after we've read the paper and had a cup of tea down here.' That's what we sometimes dream of doing.

But, of course, it would never happen. If I could convince the children to take themselves upstairs on their own, the results don't even bear thinking about. Our three-year-old would unravel the loo roll and use it to redecorate the bedrooms. Our toddler would fill up the bath and practise her 'swimming' with her characteristic and terrifying fearlessness—and the evening would end up with a call to the emergency services, property damage, insurance claims, and probably criminal charges for parental negligence.

So, instead, at 6.30 we announce that it's bedtime—and then we cajole and carry the children upstairs, run the bath, get them into it, wash them, dry them, dress them, read to them and put them to bed. As parents, we must both instruct our children in what we want them to do, and then lead them by the hand through every step of the procedure.

I mention all that because you and I, as children of our heavenly Father, need just the same from him. In our sinfulness and frailty, we *cannot* and *will not* obey his Word and do his work on our own. It simply will not happen. We will turn to our own agendas or drown in our own incompetence before we even begin. But, in his goodness, the God who calls us to serve him comes alongside us and works within us to *enable us* to serve him.

Notice how God comes alongside his people to enable them to obey the Word he speaks to them through his prophet: 'Then Haggai, the messenger of the LORD, spoke to the people with the LORD's message, "I am with you, declares the LORD"' (v. 13). The LORD is there, but it is not simply the case that he is close by, watching from the sidelines; no, he is moving in the hearts of his people: 'And the LORD *stirred up* the spirit of Zerubbabel the son of Shealtiel, governor of Judah, and the spirit of Joshua the son of Jehozadak, the high priest, and the spirit of all the remnant of the people' (v. 14a, emphasis added). Once God had done that, and only once he had done that, we see the result: 'And they came and worked on the house of the LORD of hosts, their God ...' (v. 14b).

We can often fall into the trap of teaching and believing a kind of stunted version of Christianity that begins with God's grace in saving us and then turns to a focus on works. It goes something like this: 'We were lost in our sin and condemnation, but God stepped in through Jesus, paid the price of our sin and moved our hearts to respond in faith—*we're saved by grace*; but now that we're saved, God calls us to works. So, new Christian, here is your list of instructions: read your Bible, be a godly spouse, evangelize your neighbours, serve in your local church. You have been saved by grace, so now get on with your spiritual "To do" list and put in the hard work as your fitting response to what God has done for you.'

While all that is true on one level, that summary fails to capture the dynamics of living the Christian life as the Bible portrays it. The biblical picture of the Christian life highlights God's amazing grace *from start to finish*; from taking the initiative in saving us, through calling us to himself, through giving us the power to live the Christian life, right through to taking us to be with him for ever in heaven.

Having saved us and made us his own through the blood of Jesus, God calls us to serve him, but he doesn't leave us on our own to do that part by ourselves. He comes alongside us and works within us by his Holy Spirit to enable us to do what he has called us to do through his Word. This is the reality that Paul proclaims when he writes to the Galatian Christians, 'It is no longer I who live, but Christ who lives in me. And the life I now live in the flesh I live by faith in the Son of God, who loved me and gave himself for me' (Gal. 2:20). Our ability and resources to live the Christian life and to serve the Lord Jesus flow from our union with him.

The work of rebuilding the temple only happens here because the LORD is with his people (v. 13). They only get on with it because he stirs up their spirit to do it (v. 14). Had the chapter ended at verse 12, with the people repentant in heart but powerless to obey, the temple would never have been rebuilt. But because God moved in them and empowered them to do what he called them to do, the temple was in fact built and completed.

If we know and trust the Lord Jesus, we are united to him by his Spirit who lives within us. That is why Jesus could say in Matthew 28, when he gave us our gospel assignment to go and make disciples of all nations, 'And behold, I am with you always, to the end of the age' (v. 19; words, of course, that echo Hag. 1:13).

So the reality of Jesus's empowering help and presence is something to rejoice in and give thanks for. He *is* with us and in us, so the work before us *is* possible. However, it is possible for us to limit and even undermine God's work in us and through us by his Holy Spirit. There are many ways that we can do this, but here I suggest two in particular.

The first is by damaging our fellowship with him through sin. Notice again how relational God's interactions with his people are here. The LORD sends his Word to his people by his prophet and speaks to them with personal directness. He calls them to renewed faithfulness and then makes to them the crucial commitment of verse 13 that he is with them. By his Spirit he was present with his ancient people, and since the day of Pentecost he now dwells in his people. That relationship is bound by a contract or a covenant that God makes with his people. Because Jesus, through his death, has paid the debt that we owe, and because we have the merits of Jesus accounted to us, God promises never to leave us. The Bible likens our relationship with God to a marriage; it is a permanent bond, and God will not give up on us or leave us. And just like a marriage, it is more than simply a written covenant or contract; it is a genuine and living relationship. So, just as in a human marriage, we can easily abuse the relationship or simply ignore it; and when we do, we know that our fellowship will be diminished.

If we are ignoring God and living in rebellion against him—in big ways or small ways, secret ways or open ways—we will find that the fruitfulness of our service dwindles and diminishes. If we are rebelling against him and giving way to sin in our lives, we will keep him at arm's length and limit his work in and through us. Just as when bitterness and hard-heartedness in a marriage make the marriage fruitless and joyless, so too with our relationship with God.

If you are struggling to serve and to feel motivated in gospel work, let me ask you: how is your relationship with the Lord Jesus at the moment? Are you still listening to him in his Word, talking to him in prayer, turning away from sin in obedience to him, seeking his glory, loving him and walking closely with him? Or has the marriage gone cold?

If the latter is the reality of your heart and life at the moment, the main thing you'll need to do in response to Haggai 1 is to repent and draw near to God again, so that you can enjoy the benefits and fruitfulness of the promise of verse 13 again.

That's the first way we can undermine God's gracious work in our lives: through continuing in sin and through allowing our fellowship with him to go cold. The next and related way is through prayerlessness. I don't know about you, but I find it so easy to press on with all kinds of Christian activity—to fill my diary with it until it's bursting, to wear myself out with it—but to rely on my own strength to do it and barely to pray about it. I can be a great *do-er*, but a very poor *pray-er*; and when that's the case, it is quite clear that I have bought into the proud lie that I can go it alone and do it all by myself.

But actually, if we see that we need God's presence and God's help to labour in his service, the whole exercise will be covered in prayer. Our service of God will be preceded by prayer, it will be upheld by prayer, and it will be followed up by prayer.

In a church we used to attend some years ago, the senior minister used to regularly urge us to come to the prayer meeting by reciting the same truism each month (it became a bit repetitive, perhaps, but it was exactly right). We needed to get to the prayer meeting, he told us, because 'when we work, *we work*; but when we pray, *God works*'. I wonder if you know and believe the truth of that? If you are anything like me, the odds are that your theology of prayer is rather more substantial than your practice of it!

Again, if you are struggling to find the motivation to serve and to prioritize the gospel at the moment—if you can barely find the resources to feel all that interested or concerned—why not start there and simply pray about that struggle: 'Lord, please change my heart and give me a genuine concern for your work again.'

I think that is actually exactly what the Lord is doing in Haggai 1:14. Once the LORD has affirmed that he is with his people, notice the first thing he does: he 'stirs up' the spirit of his people so that they will get to work. For their spirit to be stirred, God needed to work in them by his Spirit. How much we need his stirring in our hearts as well!

QUESTIONS FOR REFLECTION, DISCUSSION AND APPLICATION

1. Where do you see evidence that God has been moving and enabling you to prioritize his work? Rejoice in this and give thanks to him.
2. Which of the three essential elements do you sense you may have been neglecting: your hearing of God's Word, your right attitude of fear towards God, or your relationship with the God who is present with us? What have been the effects of that neglect?
3. What steps can you take this week to listen more carefully to God's Word?
4. What steps can you take this week to fear God rightly, and to adjust your attitude towards him if it has been wrong?

5. Are there particular areas of sin that you sense are damaging your fellowship with God? What steps can you take this week to address that sin?
6. Are there areas of your life and service which you have neglected to pray for? What steps can you take this week to make more of the privilege of prayer?

confessio of our hearts turn to God does that prayer

NOTES

1   This is a substantial and important subject, and developing this point fully goes beyond the scope of this book. For a helpful exploration and discussion, see Christopher Ash, *The Priority of Preaching* (Fearn/London: Christian Focus/Proclamation Trust Media, 2009).

The glorious building (2:1–9)

In the seventh month, on the twenty-first day of the month, the word of the LORD came by the hand of Haggai the prophet, 'Speak now to Zerubbabel the son of Shealtiel, governor of Judah, and to Joshua the son of Jehozadak, the high priest, and to all the remnant of the people, and say, "Who is left among you who saw this house in its former glory? How do you see it now? Is it not as nothing in your eyes? Yet now be strong, O Zerubbabel, declares the LORD. Be strong, O Joshua, son of Jehozadak, the high priest. Be strong, all you people of the land, declares the LORD. Work, for I am with you, declares the LORD of hosts, according to the covenant that I made with you when you came out of Egypt. My Spirit remains in your midst. Fear not. For thus says the LORD of hosts: Yet once more, in a little while, I will shake the heavens and the earth and the sea and the dry land. And I will shake all nations, so that the treasures of all nations shall come in, and I will fill this house with glory, says the LORD of hosts. The silver is mine, and the gold is mine, declares the LORD of hosts. The latter glory of this house shall be greater than the former, says the LORD of hosts. And in this place I will give peace, declares the LORD of hosts."'

Church of England records indicate that in its churches over the last eighty years formal church affiliation has dropped by two-thirds. Over the last fifty years, church attendance by adults has dropped by about 50 per cent, while church attendance by children has dropped by a similar percentage over the last twenty-five years.[1]

I don't know how you feel as you look at the state of gospel work locally, nationally and throughout the Western world at the moment. There are, of course, pockets of growth and life. But the broader scene in the UK and throughout the West is pretty discouraging: denominations rife with false teaching and internal conflict, massive numerical decline, and the rapid rise of Islam to fill the vacuum left by disappearing churches. We look back to better days and wonder what the future can possibly hold.

The people of Jerusalem of 520 BC were filled with despair as they surveyed the state of God's work in their day. Their immediate assignment was to rebuild the ruined temple of Jerusalem. At the start of Haggai we saw that their problem had really been lack of interest in God's building project; they were far more interested in feathering their own nests. But as God rebuked them through his prophet, their hearts were stirred (1:14) and they got to work. But now, a month on, as they turn their minds to the job at hand and survey the building site before them, and as they remember the building that once stood in its place, they are filled with despair. And the LORD knows it: 'Who is left among you who saw this house in its former glory? How do you see it now? Is it not as nothing in your eyes?' (2:3).

Of course, it did seem as nothing in their eyes because it *was*, more or less, nothing—a basic foundation, an outline in the sand, and nothing more. Those who remembered Solomon's great temple knew that, even if they could complete the building works before them, they would never be able to match the glory of the former temple.[2] So God calls the despairing people to get to work, promising that he is with them, reminding them that he made a covenant promise to stick with them, and assuring them that his Spirit remains among them (vv. 4–5).

These verses are a call for God's discouraged people to get to work doing what he has given them then, and us now, to do. But notice how God sets about getting his people to work: he gives us a vision of his glorious future to inspire, drive and shape our activity today (vv. 6–9). God's vision and plan for the future involves three elements: it begins with an almighty *shaking;* it then gives way to unimaginable *splendour*, and it results in complete *shalom*, or peace.

The first element in God's plan: a shaking

For thus says the LORD of hosts: Yet once more, in a little while, I will shake the heavens and the earth and the sea and the dry land. And I will shake all nations, so that the treasures of all nations shall come in, and I will fill this house with glory, says the LORD of hosts (vv. 6–7).

As with many of God's promises in the Old Testament, there are two levels of fulfilment of this promise that we need to consider. On the first level, there is the fulfilment of this promise that has *already* taken place in the history of Israel.

The people of Jerusalem in 520 BC faced an impossible task in the rebuilding of the temple; they were a beleaguered minority in a ruined city annexed to a great empire, and powerless within it. And God had set them the job of rebuilding one of the greatest buildings of the ancient world. Frankly, it seemed that it was all simply beyond them. It was one thing for great King Solomon to build the first temple at a time when he was ruler of a mighty kingdom; but now, for a subjugated and powerless people with no kingdom at all, it looked hopeless.

But for the God of the whole world, minor inconveniences like that were no real barrier to his plans. So he promised that he would order and reorder international events in order to fulfil his plan. He would once again give the world a good shake (v. 6) so that the treasures of the surrounding nations would tumble into the temple treasury and make the rebuilding possible (v. 7). The 'once more' of verse 6 is there to remind us of the great shaking of the earth that accompanied the giving of the law at Sinai, in the days when God performed the great miracle of salvation in bringing his people out of slavery in Egypt (Exod. 19:18). Haggai points forward to another great act of God for the good of his people. The image here is of God lifting up the surrounding nations as though they are on a sheet and shaking the four corners of that sheet until the silver and gold from those nations tumble into the centre of the sheet and land right in the temple treasury.

It all seemed unlikely at best but, in the book of Ezra, we read that during or soon after Haggai's ministry the Persian emperor Darius made an extraordinary decree that taxes levied on a neighbouring province should be used to pay for the reconstruction of the temple (Ezra 6:1–12). Again, centuries later, the Roman ruler Herod the Great poured money from the Roman treasury (albeit from taxes drawn, at least in part, from Judah) into a reconstruction of the temple on the grandest scale, making it once again one of the greatest buildings in the world. Parts of the ruin of that building (like the great Western Wall) are there in Jerusalem for all to see today as a reminder that God fulfils his promises.

So, on one level, the promise of this vision was fulfilled in the history of Israel and in the temple building. But the New Testament makes it clear that the scale of this promise was too big to be confined to the physical structure of the temple in Jerusalem. There was a greater fulfilment yet to come. With that in mind, consider the way that the writer of Hebrews picks up these words of Haggai in chapter 12 of his letter and teaches us about their ultimate fulfilment.[3] The writer has been talking about the heavenly city of Zion and he goes on to say this:

See that you do not refuse him who is speaking … now he [that is, God] has promised, 'Yet once more I will shake not only the earth but also the heavens' [quoting Hag. 2]. This phrase 'Yet once more,' indicates the removal of things that are shaken—that is, things that have been made—in order that the things that cannot be shaken may remain (Heb. 12:25–27).

What is the writer of Hebrews saying? What is his point? He is saying that God's building plan is ultimately not for an earthly structure, but for a heavenly city, one populated by people who know him through faith in the Lord Jesus Christ. The writer says explicitly that this grand plan of God's will come to ultimate fruition when he 'shakes' the heavens and the earth, removing the creation we know now, and allowing his heavenly city alone to remain in all its splendour. In light of all this, his urgent appeal to us is to see to it that we 'do not refuse him who is speaking'. A day is coming, God tells us in his Word, when he will give this world an almighty shake, and it simply will not survive. The only place that will rest secure on that day is God's city in heaven, and the only people who will be safe on that day of shaking are those who have a sure place in his city through faith in his Son. So, the writer of Hebrews tells us, *listen up*.

I was fascinated to learn that, at various points along the north Japanese coastline where the great tsunami struck in 2011, there are stones, some of them placed six hundred years ago, bearing an etched message that on no account should anyone build houses or villages any lower down that hill than where those stones are placed. Hard experience of the death and destruction caused by tsunamis (which of course are massive waves resulting from powerful underwater earthquakes) prompted the people of those communities long ago to leave lasting warnings of where disaster had struck before and where it would surely strike again. 'When the earth shakes and the waves rise, you will not survive if you build here. Any city you build in this place will be wiped out. So listen up.'

For many decades and centuries those warnings etched on stone and peppered along the coastline would have looked like downbeat, scare-mongering, fun-spoiling prophecies of doom. And many people clearly didn't take them seriously, because they did in fact build whole communities below them. But on 11 March 2011 it became clear that ignoring the warning was folly indeed.

In a similar way, Haggai 2:6–7 is God's warning to us and to our world:

'thus says the LORD of hosts: Yet once more, in a little while, I will shake the heavens and the earth and the sea and the dry land. And I will shake all nations …' Just as God had the power to shake money from the pockets of the wealthy neighbours of powerless Israel in days long gone so that the temple might be rebuilt in order to fulfil his purposes for Jerusalem below, so he has power to shake both heaven and earth and destroy everything but his heavenly city in order to fulfil his purposes for his great city above. He has committed himself to doing just that in Haggai 2, and in case we missed it, he has reaffirmed that commitment in Hebrews 12. So we must listen to the warning and heed it.

But an obvious question arises: why is God going to do this? Why will he find it necessary to shake the heavens and the earth and bring about their destruction? Surely it all seems a bit unnecessary, unpleasant and extreme. More than that, the promise here in Haggai 2 appears to be set in such a positive context; it is here to inspire us and get us to work. But surely this destructive shaking is *bad* news, not good news.

At various stages, our children have enjoyed playing with Play-Doh. You may have seen and handled the stuff (if you have small children you will be an expert on Play-Doh); it's a wonderfully mushy, doughy substance for building shapes and making pictures. It comes in a whole array of different colours, and each colour lives in its own little pot. If you've ever played with Play-Doh before, you'll know how quickly and easily the colours get mixed and blended together, and the lovely rainbow of different-coloured doughs becomes one big blob of mucky brown. At that stage there is nothing for it but to put it in the bin and start again. When I play with Play-Doh with our children I try to convince them to keep the colours separate, but it's pretty hopeless. After about two minutes it's all just mush, and the stuff is fit only for the bin.

The Bible is very clear on the fact that this world is ruined beyond fixing; we humans have ignored God's boundaries and rejected his loving rule in our lives. We'll think about that more below, but part of the result of our rejection of God's loving rule over us is mess, confusion, hurt and damage. And the evidence is everywhere. God's beautiful technicolour world is a murky brown of hurts and confusion. And so he intends to make a fresh start. He has committed himself to carrying out a great shaking that will put to an end this broken world, leaving only his perfect heavenly city. That is why this destructive shaking is such good news for his people; it will remove this sin-damaged world so that God's unspoilt heavenly city may be enjoyed in all its beauty and perfection in the new creation.

The second element in God's plan: splendour

And I will shake all nations, so that the treasures of all nations shall come in, and I will fill this house with glory, says the LORD of hosts. The silver is mine, and the gold is mine, declares the LORD of hosts. The latter glory of this house shall be greater than the former, says the LORD of hosts (vv. 7–9a).

The first temple, built by Solomon and then destroyed by the Babylonians, was both large and ornate; its walls were lined with cedar, carvings of palm trees and pomegranates decorated the doors, and even the floors were covered in gold. But God insists that 'The latter glory of this house shall be greater than the former' (v. 9).

How could that be possible? The people of Jerusalem of 520 BC were weak, defenceless, subjugated and short on cash. How was God going to pull *that* off? Well, it became possible when the Romans arrived, a few centuries later, and when the Roman puppet king in Judea, Herod the Great, made it his personal project to apply the wealth of the Roman empire to the expansion and improvement of the temple. The result was one of *the most magnificent buildings the world had ever seen*. The historian Josephus describes the sight of the great temple on approaching the city: 'covered all over with plates of gold of great weight ... at the first

Site of temple where Jesus was dedicated

rising of the sun, [it] reflected back a very fiery splendour, and made those who forced themselves to look upon it to turn their eyes away, just as they would have done at the sun's own rays.'4

What in 520 BC was a building site in the midst of a forlorn city, would, by the time of Jesus, be transformed into the most beautiful building in the Roman empire and in the world of that day. But the vision of splendour of verses 6–9 outstrips even the splendour of the amazing temple completed by Herod the Great. So if we read these verses thinking that something more must be in view, our suspicion is confirmed when we turn to the New Testament. In Revelation 21 we are given an elaboration of Haggai's prophetic vision of the future, where the vision of a renewed temple has given way to a vision of a glorious heavenly city in a new heaven and a new earth:

Then I saw a new heaven and a new earth, for the first heaven and the first earth had passed away, and the sea was no more. And I saw the holy city, new Jerusalem, coming down out of heaven from God, prepared as a bride adorned for her husband. And I heard a loud voice from the throne saying, 'Behold, the dwelling place of God is with man. He will dwell with them, and they will be his people, and God himself will be with them as their God. He will wipe away every tear from their eyes, and death shall be no more, neither shall there be mourning, nor crying, nor pain any more, for the former things have passed away …'

… And I saw no temple in the city, for its temple is the Lord God the Almighty and the Lamb. And the city has no need of sun or moon to shine on it, for the glory of God gives it light, and its lamp is the Lamb. By its light will the nations walk, and the kings of the earth *will bring their glory into it*, and its gates will never be shut by day—and there will be no night there. *They will bring into it the glory and the honour of the nations* [notice the echo of 'the treasures of the nations', Hag. 2:7]. But nothing unclean will ever enter it, nor anyone who does what is detestable or false, but only those who are written in the Lamb's book of life (Rev. 21:1–4, 22–27, emphasis added).

That is the splendid future that God has in store. That's where Haggai 2 is ultimately taking us, beyond the great shaking. It is pointing us to life in a place where tears are wiped away, where mourning, death and pain are no more—a place of such light that the sun is no longer needed, a place where people from every nation will flood in. Haggai is pointing us to a place where suffering is done away with, where children don't get ill or go without food, where loving relationships aren't severed by death, where natural disasters don't destroy homes and lives, where there is no more crying because there doesn't need to be any crying any more.

But notice how such splendour is achieved: 'But nothing unclean will ever enter it, nor anyone who does what is detestable or false, but only those who are written in the Lamb's book of life' (v. 27). All evil and every evildoer will be excluded from this splendid future in heaven because evil would spoil its perfection. The vision of such a place must be attractive to us all, but what hope does any one of us have for inclusion in this promised future? Surely, as those who do *evil things* and who are *impure* we are automatically excluded. What's the way in? How do we avoid the destruction of God's 'shaking', and how do we avoid exclusion from this splendid new creation? The answer comes at the end of those words from Revelation 21: we are included in this promised future by having our names written in the Lamb's book of life; that is, by trusting in the Lord Jesus Christ, who died as the Lamb of God, as a sacrifice, to bear the penalty of all the detestable and false things we have done and to cleanse us from the impurity of our sin.

Have you done that? Do you have confidence that your name is in his book, that your wrongdoing is cleansed, and that your future is secure? If you don't have that confidence, you certainly *can* have it, simply by turning from rebellion and trusting in the Lord Jesus and in what he has done to make this splendid future available to us. It's a gift: won for us at great cost through his death, but made freely available to us if we will receive it through faith.

God's great plan is ultimately to fill his heavenly city with his treasured possessions from all nations (Hag. 2:7), the people he has purchased at great cost through the death of his Son.[5]

The third element in God's plan: shalom

The latter glory of this house shall be greater than the former, says the LORD of hosts. And in this place I will give peace [shalom], declares the LORD of hosts (v. 9).

If you and I were in Israel today greeting friends or saying goodbye to them, our first and our final word would almost certainly be 'shalom', because 'shalom' is the basic Hebrew greeting. If you and I met each other on the streets of Tel Aviv, I would say 'shalom' to you, and you would reply by saying 'shalom, shalom'.

'Shalom' is a good word to use as a greeting because it's a word that simply means 'peace'—peace in its fullness, the kind of peace that comes from having our relationships in order and knowing that our lives are free of conflict and totally secure. But while we might wish 'shalom' for each other, our experience of peace in this world is usually short-lived. We all know that our world is a place of conflict between families, colleagues, communities and nations. Our homes, workplaces, political assemblies, sports stadiums, town centres, schools and shops—from time to time at least—are all places of conflict. However much we long for peace and strive for peace, it so often eludes us.

The Bible insists that the root cause of our conflicts with one another is our deeper and more significant lack of peace with the God who made us. God created us for a relationship with him—that we might live with him as our loving ruler and joyfully respond to his kindness with gratitude and obedience. But we don't much like living under anyone else's authority, and each of us, the Bible insists, has pushed God away and rejected his rule in our lives. In his justice, God has responded in judgement. That judgement begins as he allows us to reject his way and to taste the bitter fruit of each of us living our own way. Ultimately, though, we will see his judgement fully revealed in that coming great act of 'shaking' that Haggai speaks about, when this world will be destroyed and evildoers will be consigned to an eternity separated from God and his good gifts.

However, in his new, post-shaking creation, God promises that he will give peace, 'shalom'; that is, comprehensive well-being and settled relationships on every side (2:9). At the heart of that 'shalom' is the promise of true peace with God himself. Although we are naturally at odds with him because of our rebellion against him, and although we deserve his judgement and his rejection, he offers us peace, acceptance, and a place in his splendid future and glorious new creation through the work of his Son, the Lord Jesus Christ.

Jesus enjoyed a perfectly harmonious relationship with God the Father, but he took on himself our guilt, and so faced the rejection of his Father, crying out as he died, 'My God, my God, why have you forsaken me?' He faced the bleakness of alienation from God—the alienation we deserve—so that you and I might be reconciled to him. We don't have to buy it or earn it (indeed, we never could), but it is ours to receive. True, lasting, comprehensive peace.

It is significant that God promises to 'fill this house with glory' (v. 7). He means that he will fill the house once again with his glorious presence, which he had removed in judgement before the exile. The presence of God at the temple signalled that access to God and a right relationship with him were possible; his presence among his people in the heavenly city will be a permanent sign that a restored relationship with him has been achieved.

God's vision for the future involves a great shaking that gives way to unimaginable splendour and results in shalom—God's perfect peace. That's the glorious future vision that God sets out for his people. Now notice again why he takes the trouble to share his vision and his plans with us: 'Be strong, all you people of the land, declares the LORD. Work, for I am with you, declares the LORD of hosts' (v. 4).

Like the people of Jerusalem in 520 BC, we are living in an age of partial fulfilment of God's promises. The house is only partly built; we await the completion and things are sometimes slow-going in the work of the gospel. But God is still committed to his covenant promises (v. 5), and he is still with us, not simply in our midst by his Spirit, but now living within us. But most of all, his plans are heading for a glorious future (v. 6). In an age when it often seems that there is much cause for discouragement in gospel work, God shows us that his purposes are progressing unstoppably. He will complete his spiritual house, the church, and bring his people to the new creation. Our job is to get on with the work he has given us to do, that of making disciples of all nations by proclaiming the good news.

QUESTIONS FOR REFLECTION, DISCUSSION AND APPLICATION

1. Does the progress of the gospel seem 'as nothing in your eyes' at the moment? Do you share the discouragement that the people felt in Haggai's day? What are some particular discouragements for you as you consider the progress of the gospel today?
2. How does the vision of the 'shaking' challenge and encourage you?
3. How does the vision of the 'splendour' encourage you?
4. How does the vision of 'shalom' encourage you?
5. This future vision was given to encourage the people that they might get to work. What is the particular gospel assignment you need to get on with in light of this vision?

NOTES

1 Figures are approximate and are drawn from *Church Statistics 2010/11* (London: Archbishops' Council, Research and Statistics, Central Secretariat, 2012); available online at www.churchofengland.org.

2 MacKay rightly and helpfully observes that '[t]he comparison was not a matter of mere size. The dimensions mentioned in Cyrus' decree—ninety feet high and wide (Ezra 6:3)—compare favourably with those of Solomon's Temple—ninety feet long, thirty feet wide and forty-five feet high (1 Kings 6:2). Rather they were thinking that they could never make it like it was before in terms of its grandeur and magnificence. All the stonework had been covered with cedar panelling, and there had been gold everywhere—even on the floors (1 Kings 6:30).' John L. MacKay, *Haggai, Zechariah and Malachi: God's Restored People* (Focus on the Bible. Rev. edn.; Fearn: Christian Focus, 2003), pp. 39–40.

3 Aside from Hebrews' explicit reference to this promise with reference to the final judgement, we probably see a further partial fulfilment in the New Testament in the shaking of the earth at the time of the death of Jesus (Matt. 27:51–54).

4 Josephus, *The Wars of the Jews,* book 5, chapter 5.

5 See also Zechariah 9:16, where God's saved people are depicted as jewels on his crown.

The defiled people and the gracious God (2:10–19)

On the twenty-fourth day of the ninth month, in the second year of Darius, the word of the LORD came by Haggai the prophet, 'Thus says the LORD of hosts: Ask the priests about the law: "If someone carries holy meat in the fold of his garment and touches with his fold bread or stew or wine or oil or any kind of food, does it become holy?"' The priests answered and said, 'No.' Then Haggai said, 'If someone who is unclean by contact with a dead body touches any of these, does it become unclean?' The priests answered and said, 'It does become unclean.' Then Haggai answered and said, 'So is it with this people, and with this nation before me, declares the LORD, and so with every work of their hands. And what they offer there is unclean. Now then, consider from this day onward. Before stone was placed upon stone in the temple of the LORD, how did you fare? When one came to a heap of twenty measures, there were but ten. When one came to the wine vat to draw fifty measures, there were but twenty. I struck you and all the products of your toil with blight and with mildew and with hail, yet you did not turn to me, declares the LORD. Consider from this day onward, from the twenty-fourth day of the ninth month. Since the day that the foundation of the LORD's temple was laid, consider: Is the seed yet in the barn? Indeed, the vine, the fig tree, the pomegranate, and the olive tree have yielded nothing. But from this day on I will bless you.'

As I write, a recent drama of British political life has reached its closing chapter. A former cabinet minister who lied to the police about a speeding offence has been jailed along with his ex-wife for eight years for perverting the course of justice. It was an outcome that this former cabinet minister had desperately hoped to avoid. In a last-ditch effort to avoid jail when the case finally came to trial, he reversed the position he had maintained for ten years and admitted to the court that he had, in fact, asked his wife to claim falsely that she was driving when the speed camera caught his car. But it was far too little, far too late, and the court was unimpressed. Having lied repeatedly and persistently over the course of a decade, a hasty confession when the truth could no longer be concealed was simply insufficient to excuse his crime. If he really imagined that his belated good behaviour would cancel out some of his bad behaviour and spare him jail, he now knows better. Delusion has given way to reality.

The prophet Haggai sets out in this passage to address a similar delusion in our hearts that crops up regularly when we consider our standing before God. He shows us that no amount of good behaviour can cancel out our bad behaviour in God's sight, and no amount of good behaviour can put God in our debt.

Back in chapter 1 the prophet called the people of Jerusalem of 520 BC to leave aside their domestic concerns and get to work rebuilding God's ruined house, and, at the end of chapter 1, they did just that. Our challenge from that chapter was to reorder our priorities and to put the work of the gospel as a clear number one. We were challenged to get out our chequebooks and our diaries, and make the work of proclaiming the good news of Jesus our top priority. But here in the second half of chapter 2 the prophet Haggai has a different aim. It is to help us to think realistically about what our good works will achieve—or, better, what they *won't achieve*—in God's sight.

In particular, he highlights for us two things that our good works will never achieve in God's sight: they will never excuse our wrongdoing, and they will never earn us God's blessing.

Good works will never excuse our wrongdoing

It's 7.30 a.m. on a chilly morning in Jerusalem on the twenty-fourth day of the ninth month in the second year of King Darius, 520 BC, and Jerry the Jerusalemite has a smile on his face and a new bounce in his step.

Looking back, Jerry knows that he and his wife Becky had their priorities in a muddle for some time. They had been spending a lot of time and money on their massive and rather impressive home renovation, all the while neglecting the fact that God's temple was in ruins. So when the prophet Haggai had come on the scene three months ago and called the people of Jerusalem to get out their chequebooks and their diaries and reorder their priorities, Jerry and Becky had made a radical and costly response. They had returned their brand new sixty-five-inch TV to the department store and given the money instead to the temple fund. Jerry had gone down to part-time at work, taken a pay cut and abandoned plans for the loft conversion, all so that he could give his time to the rebuilding effort.

So here he is, 7.30 in the morning, making his way over to the building site. And he is feeling pretty good about what he and Becky have done. But as he arrives at the building site his heart sinks, because the prophet Haggai has turned up again. It was pretty uncomfortable listening to him last time he came, and here he is again, standing on one of the foundation stones of the temple, and he is obviously getting ready to speak.

Haggai begins, 'Thus says the LORD of hosts: Ask the priests about the law: "If someone carries holy meat in the fold of his garment and touches with his fold bread or stew or wine or oil or any kind of food, does it become holy?"' (vv. 11–12).

Jerry doesn't quite see what Haggai is getting at, but it's a simple question, and he knows what the priests will say: consecrated meat (meat that is ceremonially clean because it has been set apart for sacrifice) won't transfer its holiness to objects touched by the garment in which it is being carried. Holiness isn't contagious, and it isn't just passed from object to object—and certainly not second-hand. That's an easy question; 'The priests answered and said, "No"' (v. 12b).

Then Haggai said, 'If someone who is unclean by contact with a dead body touches any of these, does it become unclean?' (v. 13).

Jerry knows the answer to that question too; holiness isn't passed from one object to another, but *defilement* certainly is. If you touch a dead body (just about the most unclean thing there is in the law), its uncleanness is contagious, and everything else you touch will be made unclean. Jerry wonders where this is going, but the punch line isn't long in coming: 'Then Haggai answered and said, "So it is with this people, and with this nation before me, declares the LORD, and so with every work of their hands. And what they offer there is unclean"' (v. 14). This nation and this people are unclean in God's sight. And because they are unclean, whatever they do for the temple, and whatever they offer as a sacrifice in the temple, is defiled. It's contaminated, compromised; it's no good.

That all comes as a bit of a shock to us, and I'm sure it came as a bit of a shock to the people of Jerusalem. After all, they seemed to be doing so well. Sure, they had taken sixteen years to get moving on the temple project—and that was a bit of an embarrassment—but they were moving on it now.

It is helpful as we read Haggai to notice that he was not the only prophet of God at work in Jerusalem at this time. The prophet Zechariah was also on the scene, and his message sheds some light on what Haggai was saying. The first message from Zechariah was delivered a few weeks *after* Haggai's first message in chapter 1 and the resulting recommencement of building works, but a few weeks *before* the message that we're looking at here in chapter 2. Notice what Zechariah had to say:

Thus declares the LORD of hosts: Return to me, says the LORD of hosts, and I will return to you, says the LORD of hosts. Do not be like your fathers, to whom the former prophets cried out, 'Thus says the LORD of hosts, Return from your evil ways and from your evil deeds.' But they did not hear or pay attention to me, declares the LORD' (Zech. 1:3–4).

Weeks after the people of Jerusalem had responded to Haggai's first message and had got out their chequebooks, cleared their diaries, and put themselves out in all kinds of costly and inconvenient ways to get on with the work that God had given them to do, God sent Zechariah to call them to return to him and to urge them not to cling unrepentantly to their evil practices as their forefathers had. It is quite clear that, although the people had started to serve and to give, their hearts were still far from the Lord. We are not told what evil the people were practising, but whatever their individual sins, the people weren't yet repentant.

What they *had* done so far was to write a cheque for the temple fund; what they *had* done was volunteer some time. It may even have been quite a sacrifice for them. They were probably feeling pretty good about it. Evidently their thinking had gone a bit like this: 'I know that there is a major problem in one part of my life—an area of my life that is wrong in God's sight and that I'm not prepared to change just at the moment. I know that in some ways my heart is far from the Lord. I'm not pleased about that, but nor am I ready to deal with it. So what I'll do is this: I'll give or serve, or maybe a bit of both, and that will be enough to make God happy. Then he'll leave me alone to get on with what I was doing before.'

But here in Haggai 2, the prophet reminds them of what they already know: in the ceremonial world of Jewish ritual, clean things don't tend to make unclean things clean; but unclean things make clean things unclean very easily. So, he says, the filthy rebellion, compromise and persistent sin in your life over here contaminate any good you do over there. Your good works cannot and will not cleanse the evil in your heart before God. 'So it is with this people, and with this nation before me, declares the LORD, and so with every work of their hands. And what they offer there is unclean' (v. 14).

As we read these hard-hitting verses and try to apply them to ourselves today, we need to think precisely and clearly about what they *are* saying and what they *are not* saying to us. What these verses are *not* saying to the

Christian believer is that because I am still a sinner, God is displeased with everything I do all the time. The miracle of the good news of Jesus is that because we come to God through Jesus and through his death for us, we can actually please him. It is actually possible for sinful followers of Jesus like me and you to please God.

Consider for a moment these extraordinary words of Hebrews 13: 'Through him then [that's Jesus] let us continually offer up a sacrifice of praise to God, that is, the fruit of lips that acknowledge his name. Do not forget to do good and to share what you have, *for such sacrifices are pleasing to God*' (Heb. 13:15–16, emphasis added). The sacrifice of praise of acknowledging that we follow Jesus, and the sacrifice of doing good and sharing what we have with those in need, are pleasing to God in the believer because they are offered through Jesus, who gave his life to cleanse us from sin. God the Father delights in those things because they come to him through Jesus, even though they come from sinful people like us.

As we read Haggai 2 from this side of the cross and apply it to ourselves as Christian believers, the situation in view is not, if you like, the situation of the normal Christian life. We are all sinners until the day we die, and yet in his kindness God takes pleasure in our sacrifices of praise and works of service offered through the Lord Jesus. The situation of Haggai 2:14 is the *particular situation* of a people who are living in persistent sin and unrepentance, whose hearts are far from God, but who imagine that a bit of service here and a bit of giving there will somehow make up for it.

This is the person who gives generously to gospel work, but who at the same time treats his wife abusively and will not repent of it.

This is the teenager who always makes it to youth group on a Friday night, but whose friends at school would never in a million years guess she was a Christian by the way she behaved on a Saturday night.

This is the pillar of the monthly prayer gathering who has become a

helpful

great lover of money and has given her life over to making more and more of it by any means necessary.

___ This is the esteemed member of the church council who is known by his employees to be a tyrant and a bully.

___ This is the person who volunteers for every evangelistic outreach, but is caught up in serious sexual sin and has no intention of giving it up.

___ This is the person who serves energetically in the Sunday school and is much loved by the church, but who has a habit of heavy drinking and drunkenness, with no interest or intention of giving it up.

___ This is the person whose heart has grown cold towards the Lord Jesus, who hasn't read his Word or spent time in personal prayer in weeks, months or years, and who refuses to turn back to him, but who nonetheless keeps up a pretty good outward show of it at church.

This is the person who thinks that God will overlook her refusal to repent and the fact that her heart is a million miles away from the Lord, simply because she's written a cheque and signed up to help.

And God says, quite simply, that his standards are higher than that. The gifts and service of those who will not repent are of no value to him. Whatever they do and whatever they offer is defiled.'

Verse 14 is a warning for all of us not to fall into the illusion that as long as we're giving and serving, God allows us to live as we please. It may be a particular call to some of us to give up the pretence of a good outward show that masks a cold and unrepentant heart—and a call to return to the Lord Jesus in wholehearted repentance.

Good works can never earn us God's blessing

Now then, consider from this day onward. Before stone was placed upon stone in the temple of the LORD, how did you fare? When one came to a heap of twenty measures, there were but ten. When one came to the wine vat to draw fifty measures, there were but twenty. I struck you and all the products of your toil with blight and with mildew and with hail, yet you did not turn to me, declares the LORD. Consider from this day onward, from the twenty-fourth day of the ninth month. Since the day that the foundation of the LORD's temple was laid, consider: Is the seed yet in the barn? Indeed, the vine, the fig tree, the pomegranate, and the olive tree have yielded nothing. But from this day on I will bless you (vv. 15–19).

So far, everything has been going badly for the people of Jerusalem. They are actually experiencing God's covenant curses that he laid out in the books of Deuteronomy and Leviticus for his people if they were unfaithful. Blight, mildew and hail have ruined their crops; there is no seed in the barn; the vine, fig tree, pomegranate and olive tree have not borne fruit.

But God says that 'from this day on I will bless you' (v. 19). From this day on, he promises to give them the blessings that follow covenant obedience, instead of the curses that follow disobedience. Ah, we think to ourselves; that all makes sense, because, after all, the people have got on with the building work (1:14). Surely Haggai is saying that God is *pleased* because the building work has restarted, and so now he is going to bless the people because they deserve it. But, in reality, God is not as pleased as we might imagine, and he tells us why in 2:17: 'I struck you and all the products of your toil with blight and with mildew and with hail, yet you did not turn to me, declares the LORD.' The people had got on with some work at the temple. But their repentance had only been superficial; their hearts were still far from God. Evidently God's blessing of 2:19 is not given because he is pleased with the people. Notice, as well, the date of this blessing; it is given on the 'twenty-fourth day of the *ninth month*' (2:18, emphasis added). But the people had begun work on God's house 'on the twenty-fourth day of the month, in the *sixth month*' (1:15, emphasis added). That's exactly three months earlier. For three months the people have been giving their time and money to the temple rebuilding project—and for three months, none of their problems has gone away. In fact, the people of Israel have been experiencing God's covenant curse and not his blessing for years and years on end, ever since they laid the foundation of the temple sixteen years ago in an earlier burst of enthusiasm: 'Since the day that the foundation of the LORD's temple was laid [sixteen years ago—we know that from the book of Ezra], consider [that whole period of time]: Is the seed yet in the barn? Indeed, the vine, the fig tree, the pomegranate, and the olive tree have yielded nothing' (2:18–19a).[1]

It has been three months of renewed sacrificial giving and labour for the Lord's house, and life has improved not one jot. The same old situation persists. The Lord has not lifted his covenant curse from the people and the land. And the Lord tells them to give careful thought to that, to take note of the fact that he has not responded to their good works with blessing. And, while the Lord invites the people to ponder that fact, he then says, quite out of the blue, 'But from this day on I will bless you.'

What is God up to? What is the lesson? Why did he not bless the people back in chapter 1, on the twenty-fourth day of the sixth month, when they got on with the work? Presumably it is partly to do with the fact that the people have not turned to the Lord in their hearts (2:17). But then why does he, rather arbitrarily it seems, decide to bless them three months later, on the twenty-fourth day of the ninth month, when they clearly don't deserve it? It's all a bit puzzling initially, but the point is simple and, I think, profound.

The great lesson here is that God's blessing—his outpoured kindness—is his to give *when* and *to whom* he chooses. Back in Leviticus 26 and Deuteronomy 28 the LORD had laid out for his people a system whereby he would bless them if they obeyed him and he would curse them if they disobeyed. But the fact is that God's people were never thoroughly and wholeheartedly obedient; left to themselves, they would only call down curses and not blessings. That was true of the ancient Israelites, and the same is true of us today. So God is showing *them then* and *us now* that our good works cannot call down his blessing from heaven, because we are never thoroughly and perfectly obedient. He is showing us that there is no way for us to earn or lay claim to his kindness. And he is showing us that in his amazing mercy and generosity he can still pour out his blessing on a compromised people.

I tend to be very easily taken in by supermarket loyalty cards and I sign up for all of them. I love the thought that every time I buy a loaf of bread or a pint of milk or put fuel in my car, I am stacking up loyalty points in the bank. And it is a great feeling to collect a big pile of vouchers over a number of months and then to wander into the supermarket and present them at the till and, effectively, to say, 'I've been putting points in the bank for weeks and months, and now I'm cashing in. I'd like what's coming to me, please—my day at the theme park or my meal out at the pizza restaurant, or my free bag of groceries. I'm ready for my reward.'

It is easy for us to think that God operates some kind of loyalty system with us today. We serve, pray and give, and it's all points in our account; and then we go to him and claim our blessing. 'I'm giving generously of my money, so where's my pay increase at work?' 'I'm giving generously of my time, so where's that holiday?' 'I've done what you asked of me, now where's my blessing?'

God refuses to dance to our tune. He does not jump to when we snap our fingers. The reality is that we come to him as helpless sinners who deserve his judgement, and he graciously offers us forgiveness and acceptance through the death of his Son. Paul tells us in Galatians 3:13–14 that the Lord Jesus bore the ultimate curse of God's law by dying for us on the cross so that he might open up as a free gift the blessings of God—forgiveness, eternal life, heaven and much more besides—to everyone, Jew and Gentile, who would trust him. We can never earn or merit God's blessings, but Jesus has won them for us and offers them freely to us. Our service of him is a response of gratitude to his kindness; it does not put God in our debt.

When the people got to work in Haggai 1 and started to do the things they should have done years before, they might have expected God to shower them with riches, health, wealth and all kinds of good things. But he did nothing. The vine, the fig tree, the pomegranate and the olive tree all failed to bear any new fruit. That might have seemed strange to them. But the real shock comes at the end of 2:19; three months later, out of his sheer kindness and not because he has to, God says to a thoroughly undeserving people, 'But from this day on [from the otherwise insignificant day of my choosing] *I will bless you*' (emphasis added).

The form of that blessing might surprise the people; the blessing we read about at the end of the chapter is not health or wealth, but the fulfilment of his great kingdom promises. We will look more closely at that in our next chapter, but here in verse 19 God promises to pour out his blessings on this compromised and slow-to-obey people. And he does it simply because he chooses to.

It is important for us to hear and digest this message if we are those who are busy and feel quite stretched serving in our local churches and in other areas of gospel work. Our temptation, when we serve and give to gospel work, especially when it is a struggle to do so, is always to turn around with our hand out and expect something back from God, as if we have done him a favour. We need to hear regularly the short parable of Jesus in Luke 17 that so quickly reminds us of our rightful place:

> Will any one of you who has a servant ploughing or keeping sheep say to him when he has come in from the field, 'Come at once and recline at table'? Will he not rather say to him, 'Prepare supper for me, and dress properly, and serve me while I eat and drink, and afterwards you will eat and drink'? Does he thank the servant because he did what was commanded? So you also, when you have done all that you were commanded, say, 'We are unworthy servants; we have only done what was our duty' (Luke 17:7–10).

The most that can be said of any believer—however exemplary his or her life and service—is that he or she is an unworthy servant. The sheer unexpectedness of that final sentence of Haggai 2:19 reminds us that God's decision to shower on us the blessings of the gospel—forgiveness, acceptance, new life, the hope of heaven, the joys of being part of the Christian family and much more besides—is evidence simply of his sheer kindness. It is never anything that we can earn or deserve.

Similarly, it is important to notice the surprise of verse 19 if you find yourself slipping back into the instinctive works-righteousness thinking that we all naturally share. This kind of thinking assumes that God will somehow be impressed by the good things that we do. 'I know I'm not perfect,' we tell ourselves, 'but if I pay my taxes and am nice to my neighbour and help an old lady across the road every once in a while, surely God will owe me one.'

But the truth is that God does not owe any of us anything. He gave us the gift of life, and we have responded each one of us by pushing him away and rejecting his loving rule over our lives. What we deserve from him is judgement, but what he offers us freely through the Lord Jesus Christ are his immeasurable blessings.

QUESTIONS FOR REFLECTION, DISCUSSION AND APPLICATION

1. Have these verses surprised you? Why or why not?
2. When are you tempted to believe that God owes you his blessings? prayer
3. When are you tempted to serve or give to earn his blessings?
4. What has this passage taught you about yourself?
5. What has it taught you about God? He is terrifying
6. How do these verses prompt you to: a) repent; b) give thanks; c) serve?

NOTES

1 For further discussion of the chronology of events and the logic of these verses, see 'Going Deeper 2: The Puzzle of the Blessing of 2:19'.

The anointed King (2:20–23)

The word of the LORD came a second time to Haggai on the twenty-fourth day of the month, 'Speak to Zerubbabel, governor of Judah, saying, I am about to shake the heavens and the earth, and to overthrow the throne of kingdoms. I am about to destroy the strength of the kingdoms of the nations, and overthrow the chariots and their riders. And the horses and their riders shall go down, every one by the sword of his brother. On that day, declares the LORD of hosts, I will take you, O Zerubbabel my servant, the son of Shealtiel, declares the LORD, and make you like a signet ring, for I have chosen you, declares the LORD of hosts.'

I wonder how you would like to experience God's blessing in your life today? If you hope or pray for God to bless you, what is it that you pray for him to do? Perhaps it is a prayer for financial security, a prayer for improved health, or a prayer for healing of a broken relationship. Perhaps it is simply a prayer for strength to get through the day.

The people of Jerusalem in Haggai's day were a people in need of God's blessing. We have seen already that God had struck the work of their hands 'with blight and with mildew and with hail' (2:17); there was no seed in the barn, and there was no fruit on the vine, the fig tree, the pomegranate or the olive tree (2:19). Rather than shower the people with blessing, God had activated his covenant curses against his people because of their sin. The people of God were doubtless praying for his blessing through a restoration of their material security and prosperity.

So into these lean days, the words at the end of verse 19 must have come like a breath of fresh air: 'But from this day on I will bless you.' You can imagine the thoughts going through the minds of the people: 'Finally, our crops are going to come to something.' 'Finally, a harvest season with no hail or blight.' 'Finally, we can replace our worn-out car with something decent.' 'Finally, we can pay off the mortgage.' 'Finally, it's time for God's blessing.'

The LORD doesn't tell the people of Jerusalem *how* he will bless them at the end of verse 19. The close of that paragraph is the end of that message. At that stage Haggai stops speaking and goes home for lunch. Given the context, and given what we know about the physical, material nature of God's promised covenant blessings from the books of Deuteronomy and Leviticus, we might assume that God's blessing would involve increasing the people's crops and so on. But we are not actually told about that here.[1] The prophet simply goes home and the people are left to imagine the blessing that might be coming their way.

However, a little while later God sends his prophet Haggai back to the people for a second time that day. So far in Haggai there have been weeks and months between messages. But in verse 20 the prophet reappears and delivers to them a magnificent vision of the full and final blessing that God has in store for his people—a vision of a blessing far greater than anything they might have hoped or prayed for.

How will he do it? What will God's ultimate blessing involve? It involves two things: the elimination of his enemies and the establishment of his King.

The elimination of his enemies

The word of the LORD came a second time to Haggai on the twenty-fourth day of the month, 'Speak to Zerubbabel, governor of Judah, saying, I am about to shake the heavens and the earth, and to overthrow the throne of kingdoms. I am about to destroy the strength of the kingdoms of the nations, and overthrow the chariots and their riders. And the horses and their riders shall go down, every one by the sword of his brother' (2:20–22).

When the exiled people of Jerusalem first returned from Babylon and began to rebuild the altar of the temple in Ezra 3–4, we are told that they did their work under a dark cloud of *fear*. They wielded their shovels and pickaxes with their eyes constantly over their shoulders, not knowing which of their hostile neighbours might come to disrupt their labours or worse. 'Then the people of the land discouraged the people of Judah and made them afraid to build and bribed counsellors against them to frustrate their purpose, all the days of Cyrus king of Persia, even until the reign of Darius king of Persia' (Ezra 4:4–5).

The people of Jerusalem in Haggai's day lived a precarious existence. They were surrounded by hostile and pagan neighbours, and their city was still without walls. The memory of the horrific destruction brought by the Babylonian invasion some years before still haunted them, and they knew that if the winds shifted and the mood changed in the palace of the Persian emperor, their security and relative peace could evaporate.

Into that context of uncertainty and vulnerability God brings his promise of blessing: 'I am about … to overthrow the throne of kingdoms. I am about to destroy the strength of the kingdoms of the nations, and overthrow the chariots and their riders …' (2:21–22). God promises that he will defeat their enemies and make them completely secure.

As the years went on, the people of Jerusalem did enjoy a degree of stability and security for some time. They were able to finish reconstructing the temple and rebuilding the city, and they were able to live there in relative peace for many years. But the wholesale destruction of foreign powers and the defeat of the enemies of the people—each 'by the sword of his brother'—well, that never quite happened. To be sure, the Persian empire that ruled over Judea at this stage eventually disintegrated, but others took its place soon enough.

Whenever we see promises like this in the Old Testament that are only ever *partially* fulfilled in the history of Israel, we are always prompted to ask where the *ultimate* fulfilment lies. And we don't have to look far to see. Notice again how the promise begins: 'I am about to shake the heavens and the earth' (v. 21). Those words should sound familiar because they have appeared once before in Haggai—in 2:6: 'Yet once more, in a little while, I will shake the heavens and the earth ...'

We found before that the New Testament picks up those words and, in Hebrews 12, shows us that they speak of God's final judgement of the world: 'At that time his voice shook the earth, but now he has promised, "Yet once more I will shake not only the earth but also the heavens." This phrase, "Yet once more", indicates the removal of things that are shaken—that is, things that have been made—in order that the things that cannot be shaken may remain' (Heb. 12:26–27). In a great act of shaking, at the close of history, God will 'remove' created things—the world as we know it—so that his heavenly kingdom may remain.

In Haggai 2:7 we saw that in this great act of shaking God would draw his treasured people from every nation into his heavenly city so that they might be with him. There the shaking leads to the ultimate salvation of his people.

But now here, at the end of Haggai 2, we are taught that this same great act of cosmic 'shaking' will also simultaneously bring about the dethroning of every king but God's true King; the overturning of every kingdom that is opposed to him and his people; and the demise of every soldier who serves a foreign army. God's blessing will be seen and experienced as he eliminates his enemies.

We need to pause here and try to process this because we're not conditioned to *look for*, *hope for* and *rejoice in* the prospect of God's defeat of his enemies. We rejoice when God gives sinful people like us a changed heart and makes people who were once his enemies his friends—and it's right that we rejoice in that and give thanks for God's mercy to his enemies. After all, we who are believers were once his enemies, and apart from his mercy, verse 22 would speak of our destruction as well. But what about his eternal judgement of his enemies and his defeat of all who oppose him? Do we give thanks to him for *that*, and is *that* part of our future hope?

Many readers of this book will be living in stable Western countries. It is, perhaps, an obvious point, but we Western readers would probably read Haggai 2:22 with a rather different perspective if we were reading it in, say, Pakistan, where a recent wave of persecution against Christians has broken out in Lahore. An alleged incident of blasphemy against Muhammad prompted a mob of three thousand to torch 175 homes belonging to Christians, along with their businesses and a local church, while the call rang out from the loudspeakers of the mosque in the background, 'Kill the blasphemers'. If we were *there* reading these verses, we would more readily greet verse 22 with hope, thanksgiving and praise.

We might find it easier to see why verse 22 is such good news if we were living in Benghazi in Libya, where two Christians were recently arrested and tortured for displaying Christian symbols on their market stall. It is reported that those who tortured them used acid to burn off the crosses they had tattooed on their wrists, before electrocuting one of them, subjecting them to demeaning labour and then releasing and deporting them.

We might read these verses in a different light if we were among the Christians in Syria currently being targeted for attack, kidnap and murder by opposition forces hostile to the gospel, who are free to do their worst with no responsible and stable government in place to hold them in check.

Many believers across the world do the work of the gospel— proclaiming the good news and making disciples of Jesus Christ—all the time looking over their shoulders, waiting for enemies to come along to disrupt, persecute and even kill. God's promise here in verse 22 is of the blessing of peace and final victory, when he will remove foreign powers and kingdoms, when he will defeat the enemies of the gospel and proclaim a final victory.

Even in the Western world, in a much milder way, we know something of the weariness of facing constant opposition to the gospel. I think of an acquaintance of mine who was being interviewed for a job not long ago. When it came out in the course of the interview that he was a Christian, the woman conducting his interview said that she and her colleagues could not work alongside a Christian and apologized for wasting his time. I think of the church in Scotland that was turned out of the hotel it was due to use for its Sunday meetings because the hotel did not want to be associated with the church's unpalatable stance on gay marriage. We could think of many more examples besides. Lord Carey, the former Archbishop of Canterbury, was surely right when he commented to the BBC that Christianity is facing 'gradual marginalisation' in Britain.[2] And so for all believers in every context, verse 22 is a promise to cling to: the *constant* resistance and the *constant* tension are only for a time.

Before we move on, it's important to see that verse 22 is very definitely not an invitation to Christians to militarize and take up arms against those who oppose the gospel. Quite the opposite. Verse 22 actually liberates us from any sense that we must take it upon ourselves to defeat God's enemies for him. He will take care of that. He is the Sovereign Lord and the Just Judge.

What Jesus calls *us* to do when we face opposition is to love our enemies and pray for those who persecute us (Matt. 5:44), and we have the freedom and the security to do that because verse 22 reminds us that God has everything in hand. Ultimately, he will defeat his enemies. That is his job, and he is committed to it. So, for now, we love our enemies, not least by telling them plainly that resisting the God of the universe and rejecting his offer of forgiveness through Jesus is a terribly dangerous thing to do. And we pray that God might have mercy on them.

The establishment of his King

On that day, declares the LORD of hosts, I will take you, O Zerubbabel my servant, the son of Shealtiel, declares the LORD, and make you like a signet ring, for I have chosen you, declares the LORD of hosts (2:23).

Zerubbabel was the governor of Judah and, more significantly, a descendant of great King David. In happier times, he might well have sat on the throne of the kingdom of Judah. As it was, he served as a local governor very much under the thumb of Darius, ruler of the great Persian empire. What actual power he was allowed to exercise we don't really know. Probably Darius gave him the title 'governor' to appease the Judeans and to soften the sense of humiliation that came from being ruled over by a pagan empire. But here in verse 23 the Lord promises to increase the dignity and status of this descendant of David.

This promise that the Lord would take Zerubbabel son of Shealtiel and make him like his 'signet ring' takes on extra meaning when we learn that God had acted in judgement some years before to remove a previous Davidic ruler from the place of honour on his hand. Before the people of Jerusalem were taken into exile in Babylon, the Lord delivered this message to the Davidic king of Judah through the prophet Jeremiah:

As I live, declares the LORD, though Coniah the son of Jehoiakim, king of Judah, were the signet ring on my right hand, yet I would tear you off and give you into the hand of those who seek your life, into the hand of those of whom you are afraid, even into the hand of Nebuchadnezzar king of Babylon and into the hand of the Chaldeans. I will hurl you and the mother who bore you into another country, where you were not born, and there you shall die (Jer. 22:24–26).

God brought judgement on his unfaithful people by sending them into exile, and part of his judgement was to take the Davidic king from the place of honour and dignity on his own hand and to give him over to his enemies.

A signet ring in the ancient world acted like a signature does in today's world. Each royal house would have its own emblem or crest which would be carved into a ring and worn by the king. When the king drafted a new law or sent an edict to a far corner of his kingdom, he would stamp it with his signet, showing that the law or message carried his full authority. God treated his kings in Israel as his own 'signet rings', his official representatives, who carried his delegated authority to rule over his people Israel. But to a former king of Judah God had given the startling message of judgement that he had taken him off and set him aside. No longer would Coniah be God's signet ring, his approved ruler and representative. God made good on that promise by allowing the Babylonians to overtake the kingdom and strip the king of his authority at the time of the exile. But now, God promises, 'I will take you, O Zerubbabel my servant, the son of Shealtiel … and make you like a signet ring, for I have chosen you' (v. 23).

Why is this promise such good news? Why is it a blessing of God for his chosen leader to be established over his people?

I have found myself spending time in Haggai in a few separate bursts over the last couple of years. It so happened that I began to study these particular verses during the week when Silvio Berlusconi stepped down as prime minister of Italy at one of the low points of the Eurozone debt crisis. You may remember the sequence of events: the nation was perhaps at the lowest point of its financial crisis, its prime minister had resigned under a cloud, and for a number of days the country was leaderless. The people of Italy were a people without the direction and security that a leader must provide. It was a frightening week for that country. Since that time Italy has had a reprieve from chaos under the really quite stable premiership of Mario Monti. But he soon resigned, chaos returned, and the country suffered once more for lack of clear leadership in the wake of an inconclusive election.

A strong and established leader (if he or she is a good leader) is a gift to a nation, and God promises the blessing of an established, recognized and authoritative leader for Judah. But here is the problem: ancient Israel never again enjoyed autonomy as an independent sovereign nation. From this time on, ancient Israel would always be subject to her more powerful neighbours. Israel's leaders would never again rule over their own independent kingdom. Zerubbabel was never actually king over an independent state.

But notice the start of verse 23, which is the key: '*On that day*, declares the LORD of hosts, I will take you, O Zerubbabel my servant ...' God is going to establish his king *on that day*. He's going to do it on the day when he shakes the heavens and the earth, on the day when he draws history to a close. *On that day*, God will establish his king; he will once more choose his king and make his king like a signet ring. What is going on? How does that work?

What we need to see is that Zerubbabel, like all the kings in David's line, is ultimately only a placeholder and a representative of God's true King who would come and rule and bring in his kingdom. Throughout the Old Testament God speaks of David and his royal descendants in terms that could never be fully true of them as mere individuals, and he makes promises about what they would be and would accomplish that they would never fulfil personally. But those statements and promises were never ultimately about David or his many descendants themselves. They were in their fullest sense only about his *one great descendant*, the great Son of David, who would fulfil all God's promises for the Davidic line. All these promises about the great Davidic king—promises made to Zerubbabel included—find fulfilment in the *Lord Jesus Christ, the great Son of David*. This is the reason why Matthew, at the opening of his Gospel, takes the trouble to write down the names of all the Davidic ancestors of Jesus in his family line. Zerubbabel's name is right there in Matthew 1:12, to remind us that all these figures in history were placeholders pointing forward to God's true King.

So, how will Jesus, God's true King, be what is promised in verse 23: a *servant*, a *signet ring*, and God's *chosen one*? It will help us to answer that question if we look carefully at what Paul writes about Jesus in Philippians 2:5–11. As you read these verses, ask yourself how Jesus fulfils the promises of Haggai 2 to be God's *servant*, *signet ring* and *chosen king*.

Have this mind among yourselves, which is yours in Christ Jesus, who, though he was in the form of God, did not count equality with God a thing to be grasped, but made himself nothing, taking the form of a servant, being born in the likeness of men. And being found in human form, he humbled himself by becoming obedient to the point of death, even death on a cross. Therefore God has highly exalted him and bestowed on him the name that is above every name, so that at the name of Jesus every knee should bow, in heaven and on earth and under the earth, and every tongue confess that Jesus Christ is Lord, to the glory of God the Father.

Think of the promise in Haggai that God's King would be like his '*signet*' ring—his stamp, his official representative. Jesus is 'in the form of God' (Phil. 2:6). He is God's perfect representation to us. He is so conformed to the image of the one true God that in looking at him we see God himself. He doesn't just carry God's seal; he *is* God's seal, stamp and very being. 'I will make you like a signet ring,' God says.

God's King is his '*servant*', we read in Haggai. Jesus (Phil. 2:7) took the very nature of a 'servant' in becoming man and dying on the cross, serving his people by paying the penalty of our sin (see also Mark 10:45).

God says of his King in Haggai that he will be his '*chosen*' one. Notice the way that God the Father honours Jesus and sets him apart: 'Therefore God has highly exalted him [through raising him from the dead and exalting him to heaven in the ascension] and bestowed on him the name that is above every name ...' (Phil. 2:9).

But the ultimate purpose and end goal of this is yet to be realized and fulfilled; God has raised Jesus 'that at the name of Jesus every knee should bow, in heaven and on earth and under the earth, and every tongue confess that Jesus Christ is Lord, to the glory of God the Father' (Phil. 2:10–11). When will Jesus, God's chosen King, his true representative, his Servant, be acknowledged and honoured by all people everywhere? It will be 'on *that* day' (Hag. 2:23), on the day when God will 'shake the heavens and the earth' (2:21). It will be the day when Jesus returns to judge the world, and when his enemies will be eliminated.

As Christian believers, we know that Jesus is God's appointed King and that we must honour him. But the Lord Jesus is a King whom we cannot see and whom most people around us reject and deride. His kingdom appears in many parts of our world, and in our own experience, to grow slowly and to face constant opposition. And so we who are trusting in Jesus await the day when God will *fully and finally, publicly and powerfully*, establish the Kingship of Jesus over all the universe. And in that day, as every knee bows and every tongue confesses that Jesus is King, we his people will rest secure. In that day, our faith will become sight. In that day, our trust, hope and service of the King who is presently unseen will be vindicated before all people.

That is the great blessing God has in store for us if we're trusting in his Son. That's how he shows us his ultimate kindness. And so the implication is simply this: be encouraged, be filled with hope and not despair, and keep trusting and serving King Jesus. God sent the prophet Haggai to his people to prompt and convince them to press on with the temple project even when things looked thoroughly bleak. You and I today need to keep on serving King Jesus by living for him and telling others the urgent good news, even when things appear pretty bleak for the kingdom of God. We will only do it if we really believe that God will pour out his blessing upon us by eliminating his enemies and establishing his King.

QUESTIONS FOR REFLECTION, DISCUSSION AND APPLICATION

1. Do you find it difficult to see God's destruction of his enemies as a blessing for his people? Why or why not?
2. Why is God's destruction of his enemies really a blessing for his people?
3. Why is it such good news that God has established and will establish Jesus as King?
4. What are the kinds of blessings we tend to long and pray for?
5. How should these three verses shape the things we long and pray for?
6. In what other ways should these verses change our praying and our priorities this week?

NOTES

1   Although note the measure of tangible blessing that God does bring through the restoration of the temple and the temple system; see Ezra 6:13–22.
2   'Lord Carey Warns "Christianity marginalised"', 11 February 2012, BBC; at http://www.bbc.com/news/uk-england-devon-16995239 (accessed 19 May 2014).

Going deeper 1: Reading old-covenant blessings and curses today

Twice in Haggai 1 the LORD invites his people to 'consider your ways' (vv. 5, 7), that is, to think about how they are living and how things are working out for them. He wants them, in particular, to consider their economic situation: they are working hard, but seem to be merely getting by (v. 6); agricultural conditions are bad and crops are poor (vv. 10–11). What is the cause? The LORD wants the people to know that he himself has brought a time of leanness upon them:

You looked for much, and behold, it came to little. And when you brought it home, I blew it away. Why? declares the LORD of hosts. Because of my house that lies in ruins, while each of you busies himself with his own house … I have called for a drought on the land and the hills, on the grain, the new wine, the oil, on what the ground brings forth, on man and beast, and on all their labours (vv. 9, 11).

The people obviously had not put two and two together, but a careful reading of Haggai 1:1–11 in light of Leviticus 26 and Deuteronomy 28 shows that the LORD is holding back their prosperity in accordance with his promised covenant curses. Under the Mosaic covenant the LORD promised to bless the people and the land if they obeyed the covenant and remained faithful to it, and he promised to curse the people and the land if they disobeyed. The building of the temple was more or less the prerequisite for the proper functioning of the covenant relationship between God and his people, and so if the people neglected the temple, they were in breach of the covenant. Added to that, their inattention to the temple made it quite clear that they were not particularly interested in the healthy function of the covenant. So God enacted his promised covenant curses against them.

Notice how closely the promised curses of Leviticus and Deuteronomy resemble the experience of the returned exiles in Haggai 1:6–11: 'But if you will not listen to me and will not do all these commandments, if you spurn my statutes, and if your soul abhors my rules … then I will do this to you: … your strength shall be spent in vain, for your land shall not yield its increase, and the trees of the land shall not yield their fruit' (Lev. 26:14–16, 20). Similarly, 'The LORD will send on you curses, confusion, and frustration in all that you undertake to do … And the heavens over your head shall be bronze, and the earth under you shall be iron. The LORD will make the rain of your land powder. From heaven dust shall come down on you until you are destroyed' (Deut. 28:20, 23–24).

The reason for the people's difficulty in Haggai 1:1–11 is that God has enacted his covenant curses against them. That much is clear. What is less immediately clear is how we, as Christian believers today living this side of the cross, may read and apply these verses to ourselves. We spent time in Chapter 1 considering how the call to build the house may be transposed to a call today, under the new covenant, to fulfil the Great Commission. But what about the covenant curses? Is the enactment of these curses merely of historical interest for us, or do these verses still address us as God's people and contain for us a warning and a rebuke today? And, if so, what is the message for us?

When we encounter the curses of the old covenant and seek to read and apply sections of Scripture that speak of them, we need to tread carefully and think in terms of the broad sweep of God's salvation plans revealed through the whole of Scripture. We need to think carefully because it is vital that we do not fall into the trap of imagining that we Christian believers today could fall under God's covenant curse (we cannot, as we will see below). But we need also to avoid the opposite danger of thinking that sections of Scripture like Haggai 1:6–11 have nothing at all to say to us. After all, the events in the lives of the Old Testament people of God were written down 'for our instruction' and their judgement serves as a warning to us (1 Cor. 10:11), and we know that 'all Scripture is … profitable' (2 Tim. 3:16) for the people of God today.

To work our way through this issue, it is worthwhile to go back to basics for a moment and consider the nature of the covenant relationship between God and his people in the days of Haggai and the nature of the covenant relationship between God and us today. On one level, much is the same today as it was then. God's people then really were his people, and we today are his people. They were spiritual descendants of Abraham and of the covenant he was given in Genesis 12:1–3 (and Gen. 15:1–6) if they trusted in God's promises, just as we believers are spiritual descendants of him and his covenant today (see Rom. 4). So there is a strong line of continuity between their situation then and our situation now.

But the New Testament makes it clear that much has changed since the days of Haggai, and we should expect there to be some elements of discontinuity between their situation and ours. The Lord Jesus has come and died for our sins and given us his Holy Spirit. Through his death he has put in place a 'new covenant' and made the old covenant 'obsolete' (Heb. 8:13). The old covenant that is made 'obsolete' is not the foundational covenant with Abraham, but the secondary covenant that God made with his people at Mount Sinai in the days of Moses. That covenant, which was like a sub-section of the broader and permanent covenant with Abraham, governed how God's people would relate to him for a time, from Sinai until the coming of Jesus. This covenant, sometimes referred to as 'the law' in Scripture, included the promised blessings and curses of Leviticus 26 and Deuteronomy 28.

Paul tells us in the book of Romans that Jesus is the 'end' or 'fulfilment' (Greek *telos*) of the 'law', meaning the Sinai covenant (Rom. 10:4; both concepts of end-point and ultimate promise-fulfilment seem to be in view here). So we should expect that Jesus brings to an end, and himself fulfils, the blessings and curses of that legal framework.

Let's now take a closer look at the elements of *continuity* and *discontinuity* between the situation of God's people in Haggai 1 and our situation now with regard to the covenant curses. It is helpful in this case to reverse the order and begin with *discontinuity* before moving on to *continuity*.

Discontinuity: Jesus is the 'end' of the law

We sense that there must be some discontinuity here when we notice the fact that the New Testament never picks up the idea of the covenant curses to tell us that God is placing us, his people, under a curse. From a casual reading of the New Testament we sense pretty quickly that this simply does not seem to happen any more. It does not appear to resonate with the life and experience of the people of God under the new covenant. And there is a reason for that: Jesus is the end-point/promise-fulfilment (Rom. 10:4) of the law's blessings and curses.

One of the most arresting statements of a divine curse found outside the longer lists of blessings and curses of Deuteronomy 28 is in Deuteronomy 21:22–23. Here we are told that a person who has been hanged 'on a tree' for a capital offence 'is cursed by God'. Paul picks up this verse in Galatians 3. He reminds us that all of us would rightly invoke God's curse against us if our acceptance before him was based on our ability to keep the law (Gal. 3:10, citing Deut. 27:26). He then brings us the liberating news that we are spared the curse we rightly deserve because someone else has taken the divine curse for us: 'Christ redeemed us from the curse of the law by becoming a curse for us—for it is written, "Cursed is everyone who is hanged on a tree" [citing Deut. 21:22–23]—so that in Christ Jesus the blessing of Abraham might come to the Gentiles, so that we might receive the promised Spirit through faith' (Gal. 3:13–14).

At the cross, Jesus took on himself his people's guilt for failure to keep the law and 'become' the curse of the law. In his death he absorbed the curse fully. This brought an 'end' to the curse because its penalty was exhausted in his death. But, more than that, Jesus opened up the blessings of the covenant to his people. In this sense he brought the 'fulfilment' of those blessings to his people. It is striking that the old-covenant blessings for obedience established for a time what we might today call a 'prosperity gospel'. A faithful and obedient Israel would be a prosperous and fruitful Israel. The experience of God's blessing for obedience (limited as it was because the people's obedience was limited) acted as a prophetic visual aid, showing the Israelites and the nations what it looked like to live in God's land enjoying his bountiful blessings. Ultimately, it was a visual aid pointing to heaven.

Jesus lived a life of perfect obedience to the Father and merited fully the blessings of God. Through his perfect obedience, he has secured for his people the blessing of God, which is experienced now through our union with Christ and membership of his family on earth, and which will be experienced in its fullness in the new creation for all eternity. It is this theology of blessing that stands behind Paul's elated description of the privileges belonging to the believer in Ephesians 1:

Blessed be the God and Father of our Lord Jesus Christ, who has blessed us in Christ with every spiritual blessing in the heavenly places, even as he chose us in him before the foundation of the world, that we should be holy and blameless before him. In love he predestined us for adoption as sons through Jesus Christ, according to the purpose of his will, to the praise of his glorious grace, with which he has blessed us in the Beloved. In him we have redemption through his blood, the forgiveness of our trespasses, according to the riches of his grace, which he lavished upon us, in all wisdom and insight making known to us the mystery of his will, according to his purpose, which he set forth in Christ, as a plan for the fullness of time, to unite all things in him, things in heaven and things on earth (Eph. 1:3–10).

So there is discontinuity between the situation of the old-covenant believers in Haggai's day and our situation today when it comes to the curses of the covenant. Jesus has brought fulfilment to the blessings and curses of the covenant, absorbing the curse and opening up to his people eternal blessing. Therefore, when we read of the curses that the people experienced then, we must not fear that we too could fall under God's curse. If we are in Christ, the curse is gone and only blessing remains for us. Haggai 1 should prompt us to rejoice in the work of Jesus for us and the grace and mercy he has shown us. We should also be very clear about the fact that, although the people could expect God's material curse to be lifted and his material blessing restored if they obeyed him under that covenant situation, there is no expectation under the new-covenant situation that covenant obedience will lead directly to material prosperity.[1]

Continuity: God disciplines his children

Having said that there is significant discontinuity between the situation then and the situation now, it is important to see that there are also lines of continuity. At this point it is helpful to stand back and consider God's original purpose in using his covenant curses. They were partly prophetic in pointing forward to the work and achievement of Christ, and that purpose is now fulfilled. They were also, in significant part, tools of discipline designed to call his people to repentance and renewed faithfulness.

Notice the progression of God's application of the covenant curses in Leviticus 26. If the people break the covenant, God promises to send illness to them, leanness to their crops, and victory to their enemies—and many more curses besides—in increasing severity (Lev. 26:14–22). The LORD then says, 'And if by this discipline you are not turned to me but walk contrary to me, then I also will walk contrary to you, and I myself will strike you sevenfold for your sins' (26:23–24). The LORD then promises to bring more curses against his people if they will not repent, saying again, 'But if in spite of this you will not listen to me, but walk contrary to me, then I will walk contrary to you in fury, and I myself will discipline you sevenfold for your sins' (vv. 27–28). If the people will not turn, he promises an ultimate curse of removal from the land: 'And I will scatter you among the nations, and I will unsheathe the sword after you, and your land shall be a desolation, and your cities shall be a waste' (v. 33).

The curses are tools of discipline that God uses to bring his people to repentance; they build up gradually, and only lead to exclusion from the land as a last resort. The aim is always to bring the people back from the brink before they experience the ultimate curse of exclusion. God's aim is expressed at the end of the chapter: 'But if they confess their iniquity and the iniquity of their fathers … then I will remember my covenant with Jacob, and I will remember my covenant with Isaac and my covenant with Abraham, and I will remember the land' (vv. 40, 42).

In applying his covenant curses in Haggai's day, God was intervening sovereignly in the circumstances of his people to get their attention and to call them to repentance. He was disciplining them. Although God does not apply covenant curses as tools of discipline under the new covenant, he does still act in his sovereignty to discipline his people. That 'discipline', under the new covenant, is now purely a tool of education and training in righteousness. Its character is not that of punishment (in the sense of retribution or payment for sin) because Jesus has borne fully the punishment for our sin. The writer to the Hebrews reminds the Christians he addresses of the work of God in 'disciplining' his children in Hebrews 12. Reflecting on an unspecified struggle they are facing 'against sin' (which seems in the context to be sinful opposition against them as the people of God, 12:3–4), he writes,

And have you forgotten the exhortation that addresses you as sons? 'My son, do not regard lightly the discipline of the Lord, nor be weary when reproved by him. For the Lord disciplines the one he loves, and chastises every son whom he receives [quoted from Prov. 3:11–12].' It is for discipline that you have to endure. God is treating you as sons. For what son is there whom his father does not discipline? If you are left without discipline, in which all have participated, then you are illegitimate children and not sons. Besides this, we have had earthly fathers who disciplined us and we respected them. Shall we not much more be subject to the Father of spirits and live? For they disciplined us for a short time as it seemed best to them, but he disciplines us for our good, that we may share his holiness. For the moment all discipline seems painful rather than pleasant, but later it yields the peaceful fruit of righteousness to those who have been trained by it (Heb. 12:5–11).

God continues to act in his sovereignty to arrange the circumstances of his people for the sake of our discipline. That does not mean, of course, that in every difficulty we face we should see God acting in discipline to call us to repentance (indeed, in the context of Hebrews 12, it does not appear that the discipline of God was designed specifically as a corrective to sin, but rather as a spur towards righteousness). But it does mean that, when we face trial and difficulty, it is still spiritually healthy and prudent to heed the instruction of Haggai 1:5, 7 to 'consider your ways'. We will not find that God has enacted a covenant curse against us; those curses are done away with in Christ. But it is possible that God, in his sovereign rule of all things, is arranging our circumstances in such a way as to bring trial and frustration into our lives, in order that we might turn from sin and return to him. As we consider the question, we may conclude that God is not doing that in our particular trial (although he will still be at work in that trial to train us through it); but we may recognize that he is calling us to turn from sin in some particular area, and we may find that we are moved to repentance and renewed faith. And so it remains right and healthy, as children of the heavenly Father, to continue to heed the call to 'consider our ways'.

Going deeper 1

NOTES

1   Indeed, the 'prosperity gospel' that has done so much damage to the church throughout the majority world and, increasingly, in the West, rests in part on a fundamental misunderstanding of the new-covenant situation. It assumes that the promises of material blessings for obedience and faithfulness, which were in effect under the old covenant, still apply in material terms today. But that understanding, as we have seen already, fails to appreciate the implications of Jesus's work at the cross for the covenant curses and blessings. In particular, it fails to appreciate the prophetic nature of the old-covenant material blessings, acting as pictures of the eternal blessings that Jesus secured for his people through his obedience.

Going deeper 2: The puzzle of the blessing of 2:19

The puzzle

Haggai 2:10–19 has proved a difficult passage for commentators and preachers to deal with. On first reading, parts of it seem out of place. Consider the wider context. Haggai begins with a rebuke for the people due to their inattention to God's house in Jerusalem and brings the stark message that God has enacted his covenant curses on the people for their unfaithfulness (1:1–11). The people then respond to the message by getting on with the work before them (1:12–15). Since God's covenant curses (see Lev. 26; Deut. 28) have fallen on the people because of their disobedience, they might now expect his blessing to come on the heels of their obedience. We are not told specifically about covenant blessings, but in his next message God lays before the people a magnificent vision of his future plans for his heavenly city (2:1–9). It almost seems that, because God's people have finally got on with the temple project, God is now prepared to move his glorious plans forward. We are still waiting to hear about the blessings we might anticipate when the bombshell of 2:10–19a comes: the people of Jerusalem are defiled in God's sight (2:14) because they have not returned to him (2:17). As if that were not puzzling enough, God then announces that he is going to bless the people anyway (2:19b).

Some proposed solutions

These verses (2:10–19) have proved sufficiently puzzling that a number of creative solutions have been proposed to try to smooth things over. The first solution given is the most radical. A number of commentators suggest that part of the passage is actually in the wrong place. They propose that somewhere along the way, scribes who were copying out the book of Haggai got a bit sleepy or confused and managed to move a block of verses from chapter 1 over here to chapter 2. If the promise of blessing in 2:15–19 originally came, say, just after the people had got back to work in 1:14–15, that might make a great deal more sense. The people had got on with the work, and so blessing followed immediately (there is then a wide range of explanations for the later rebuke in 2:10–14). But the problem with that solution is that there is no evidence at all from the manuscript records to suggest that this has taken place. It is entirely speculative, and so really just a convenient way to get round a hard bit of interpretation.

Another, less radical, solution is that these verses point to an otherwise unknown relaying of the foundation of the temple. Although the foundation had been laid sixteen years earlier amid great celebration (Ezra 3:10–13), the suggestion is that somehow that foundation was no longer in place or was severely damaged, and so here in Haggai 2:18 we have record of another laying of the foundation. Under that logic, the people were still defiled and cursed up until 2:14 because they had not really made much progress on the temple, but now that the foundation is laid (2:15 onwards?), they are in favour with God and he lifts his curse and pours out his blessing (2:19b). But it seems very unlikely indeed that stone foundations of a massive building like the temple would crumble or disappear over the course of sixteen years. Moreover, it seems very unlikely that, had they been destroyed during that period, there would be no mention of it here in Haggai or anywhere else.

The opportunity of Bible puzzles

I find it very helpful to remember that the puzzling bits of the Bible provide tremendous opportunities for me to grow in my understanding.[1] After all, I am a sinner whose thinking is damaged in all kinds of ways by my sinfulness. I will bring to my reading of the Bible all kinds of assumptions that are imported from the unbelieving world and from my sinful heart, and many of these will be distorted and simply wrong. On the other hand, God's Word, the Bible, is 'perfect', 'right', 'pure', 'clean', 'true' and 'righteous altogether' (Ps. 19:7–9). So when I come to a part of the Bible that doesn't seem to make sense to me, my assumption should be that my thinking is wrong and needs to be set right. So it is a time of opportunity! And I can pray with the psalmist, 'Open my eyes, that I may behold wondrous things out of your law' (Ps. 119:18). I take it, then, that the puzzles of Haggai 2:10–19 present us with a tremendous opportunity to change our thinking and to make it more biblical.

The proposed solution: take the text as it stands!

If we take the text as it stands, the two big things that puzzle us are, first, that God still has hard words to say to a people who seem to be moving in the right direction, and, second, that he nonetheless decides to bless them. We naturally expect God to be pleased with the good things we do and we expect blessing to follow obedience. But the puzzle here leads to a surprise that challenges our presuppositions: God's blessing and the people's obedience are not linked in this case. We see from 2:20–23 that the blessing of verse 19 is ultimately the blessing of Jesus's arrival and kingly rule. So it is no surprise, perhaps, that in the giving of this blessing, God moves beyond the laws of Leviticus and Deuteronomy to their fulfilment in Jesus.

Paul teaches us in Romans 7 that the Old Testament law could never actually make us obedient on its own; all it could ever do was highlight our sin (Rom. 7:7–12). In that sense, the Old Testament law acted as the 'guardian' of God's people, pointing out their sin and leading them to the Saviour, so that they could be justified by faith in him (Gal. 3:23–25). Here in Haggai 2 the people of God were learning once again the painful lesson that they could never obey God with perfect consistency from the heart and so merit his blessings. They were learning the lesson that Isaiah learned in his day, that 'all our righteous acts are like filthy rags' (Isa. 64:6, NIV). They had been sent into exile for their unfaithfulness, and even though they were back in the land, their hearts had not really changed, and they still merited God's curse and not his blessing. That very lesson actually points us to the Lord Jesus, who is the only one who was perfectly obedient to the Father and the only one who deserved his blessing. If God's people were ever to experience God's blessing and not his curse, they would need him to step in and do something extraordinary. They would need the Saviour to come.

That fact is confirmed in the next surprise of this passage when God announces his blessing out of the blue. If God is going to bless *this* people, this unclean and unacceptable people, it must be on the basis of something other than their good works. And so it is. The blessing he has in store for them is the fulfilment of his promise of a Davidic Messiah who would establish his rule through his perfect life, sin-bearing death and glorious resurrection. The promise would come as Jesus lived that perfect life of obedience, meriting fully God's blessing, and then bearing the curse of the law in the place of his law-breaking people, opening up God's blessing to them.

A further smaller puzzle of the text is how these verses relate to the original laying of the foundation of the temple sixteen years before and to the recent progress on the building work since Haggai 1:14–15. As the text is generally rendered in English, the people are invited to consider 'onward' from the day of this oracle ('this day', 2:15, 18). But the Hebrew term rendered 'onward' could equally be rendered 'backward' (as noted in the ESV footnote), so that the people are being invited to look back over recent history and consider how things have been going for them. This seems more likely and makes better sense of the text. So in 2:15 the people are invited to 'consider from this day backward' and to ask how they fared 'before stone was placed upon stone in the temple'. This presumably refers to the days before recent building work upon the foundation that began in Haggai 1:14–15 (although it could look back even further to the days, sixteen years before and more, even before the foundation had been laid). Before they got to work on the temple, they still experienced God's curse. Then they are invited, verse 18, to 'consider from this day backward … Since the day that the foundation of the LORD's temple was laid' and to notice that over that whole sixteen-year period, God's curse had been active against them. Whether they got on with building or continued to ignore God's work, they experienced God's curse and not his blessing all the same. They were meant to see from that the simple truth that they did not deserve to be blessed. Having shown the people that even their best efforts merit curse and not blessing, the LORD then blesses the people anyway, highlighting all the more his extraordinary grace in giving his blessing to the undeserving in 2:19b.

NOTES

1 If I remember rightly, I believe I first understood this through the teaching of Phillip Jensen. I do not recall exactly where I heard or read it, but Jensen makes the same point in this article on the miracles in John's Gospel: http://phillipjensen.com/articles/miracles-in-john/ (accessed 6 April 2013).